Arthur Beilby Pearson

The new Factors Act annotated

With an introductory sketch of the origin and growth of the statutory law

Arthur Beilby Pearson

The new Factors Act annotated
With an introductory sketch of the origin and growth of the statutory law

ISBN/EAN: 9783337113049

Printed in Europe, USA, Canada, Australia, Japan

Cover: Foto ©Suzi / pixelio.de

More available books at **www.hansebooks.com**

THE

NEW FACTORS ACT

Annotated.

With an Introductory Sketch of the Origin and Growth of the Statutory Law as affecting Merchants, Bankers and others in their dealings with Mercantile Agents.

WITH AN APPENDIX OF THE STATUTES.

BY

ARTHUR BEILBY PEARSON-GEE, B.A.,
Of the Inner Temple, Barrister-at-Law,
JOINT EDITOR OF "BENJAMIN ON SALE," AND JOINT AUTHOR OF "THE FACTORS ACTS, 1823 TO 1877."

LONDON:
WILDY AND SONS,
LINCOLN'S INN ARCHWAY, W.C.,
Law Booksellers and Publishers.
MANCHESTER: MEREDITH, RAY & LITTLER.
1890

LONDON:
C. F. ROWORTH, GREAT NEW STREET, FETTER LANE, E.C.

TABLE OF CONTENTS.

	PAGE
I. INTRODUCTORY	1
(i.) Factors Act, 1823	9
(ii.) Factors Act, 1825	9
(iii.) Factors Act, 1842	12
(iv.) Factors Act, 1877	16
II. THE FACTORS ACT, 1889	19
III. APPENDIX No. 1:	
Law of France and Germany	73
IV. APPENDIX No. 2:	
Larceny Act, 1861	75
V. APPENDIX No. 3:	
Text of the Factors Acts, 1823—1877	78
VI. INDEX	91

THE NEW FACTORS ACT.

I.—INTRODUCTORY.

The consolidation in simple and comprehensible form of the law hitherto dispersed throughout the several statutes known as the Factors Acts, and the numerous judicial decisions upon the construction of those enactments, is a benefit alike to the mercantile classes and to the legal profession. The new Factors Act, which will come into operation upon the 1st of January, 1890, is intituled "An Act to amend and consolidate the Factors Acts." It will be found to substantially confirm, but at the same time in some not unimportant respects to amend, the previously-existing law, the condition of which must, therefore, form the subject of some preliminary inquiry.

The law upon this subject was formulated in the series of four Factors Acts passed in the years 1823, 1825, 1842, and 1877 respectively (a); and was defined and illustrated in a number of judicial decisions given in cases arising under those statutes. The first Factors Act (4 Geo. IV. c. 83) was, as we shall presently show, the outcome of a prolonged struggle between the Parliamentary representatives of the commercial classes and the legal profession; as a consequence of which it was merely tentative in character, and had a very narrow scope; while the three later enactments (6 Geo. IV. c. 94; 5 & 6 Vict. c. 39; and 40 & 41 Vict. c. 39),

---

(a) The text of these statutes, now repealed, is given in Appendix No. 3, *post*, pp. 78 *et seq.*

although wider in scope and progressive in application, were so hurriedly passed, in order to relax the strictness of recent judicial interpretation, or to supply some *casus omissus* in the earlier Acts, that they failed to establish the law on any clear or comprehensive basis. Hence the interpretation of these statutes often involved great difficulty and labour, and many of the reported judgments dealing with this branch of the law are masterpieces of logical analysis and luminous exposition (*a*).

Again, the earlier legislation was marked by two conspicuous blemishes. In the first place, its scope was not precisely defined, so that it was left for judicial interpretation to decide what class or classes of persons were intended to be within its operation, and a large body of case-law was wholly due to this absence of statutory definition. Secondly, the three earliest enactments were expressed in language so loose and ambiguous that judicial interpretation was again needed to determine whether or not the same class of persons was within the contemplation of the successive statutes, and another considerable body of case-law was the result.

The aim of the new Act is to remedy these defects in the earlier legislation. A preliminary section contains a series of definitions, which serve to mark out with some precision the scope and subject-matter of the statute; and in the process of consolidating within a moderate compass the provisions of the previous Acts the draftsman has substituted for the former prolixity or ambiguity of expression a terse and uniform phraseology.

We propose to inquire somewhat in detail into the provisions of the new Factors Act, and to preface our inquiry

---

(*a*) We may cite in particular, as perhaps the best-known examples, the judgment of Mr. Justice Willes in *Fuentes* v. *Montis*, and of Lord Blackburn in *Cole* v. *North Western Bank*.

with a brief sketch of the origin and growth of the statutory law relating to factors. We believe that some acquaintance with the historical side of the subject is a necessary pre-requisite for a comprehension of the existing rules of law, and venture to think that the retrospect may possess some special interest at the present time.

In the origin of the Factors Acts we have a remarkable illustration of the authority of precedent, or what Bentham irreverently termed "judge-made law," in English jurisprudence. It has been said that "a precedent embalms a principle"; in English law it sometimes creates one. A judgment at *nisi prius*, delivered on the spur of the moment, and amid the hurry of judicial business, imperfectly or even inaccurately reported (for law reporting a century and a-half ago was not an exact science), may be the source whence the current of legal decisions "broadens as it flows," until legislative interference alone can remedy the resulting evils.

In the year 1743, Chief Justice Lee, sitting at Guildhall, decided the case of *Paterson* v. *Tash*. The verbatim report of his judgment, as given in Strange (*b*), is as follows: "That though a factor has power to sell, and thereby bind his principal, yet he cannot bind or affect the property of the goods by pledging them as a security for his own debt, though there is the formality of a bill of parcels and a receipt. And the jury found accordingly." This decision, although its authority is open to serious doubt (*c*), was accepted without dispute as establishing the

---

(*b*) 2 Strange, 1178.

(*c*) There are strong reasons for maintaining that the report of *Paterson* v. *Tash* was erroneous, and that it was in fact no authority for the rule which it was assumed to have laid down. The words in the reported judgment, "though there is the formality of a bill of parcels and a receipt," point to the probability of the case being one of collusion, or, at any rate, one in which the pledgee knew that the person he was dealing

principle that at common law a factor has no power to pledge the goods of his principal, so that the latter can recover them even from an innocent pledgee who acted in ignorance of the real character of the factor. We are surprised to discover that so important a decision remained unnoticed for half a century, and that no reference is made to it in contemporary text books or reports; but in 1794 (*d*) we find the rule in *Paterson* v. *Tash* recognized and acted upon; and although many eminent judges, including Gibbs, L. C. J., Lord Eldon, Lord Kenyon, and Lord Ellenborough, expressed their disapproval of the rule—Lord Eldon, indeed, on one occasion, going so far as to disregard it (*e*)—its authority by the beginning of the present century was firmly established. Moreover, the principle, in spite of strenuous efforts to engraft exceptions upon it, was extended from the original case of a factor pledging the actual goods of his principal, to that of a pledge of a bill of lading or of other indicia of property (*f*), the extreme limit of its application being reached in cases where the factor had applied the advances made to him on

with was a factor, for otherwise there was no occasion for the formalities referred to. The parties had in fact endeavoured to effect a pledge under colour of a sale. If this be the correct view of the decision, it is clear that *Paterson* v. *Tash* was no authority for the subsequent cases, in all of which the pledgee acted honestly and without notice that the borrower was a factor. No instance can be found earlier than *Paterson* v. *Tash* where the title of an innocent pledgee was impeached. This view of *Paterson* v. *Tash* was very ably maintained by Mr. Freshfield, who represented the petitioning bankers and merchants before the Select Committee of the House of Commons, in 1823. Through the courtesy of Mr. Justice Kekewich the present writer has had an opportunity of perusing a copy of the address delivered by Mr. Freshfield before the Committee. It may be mentioned that Gibbs, L. C. J., stated, shortly before his death, that *Paterson* v. *Tash* was misreported, but unfortunately assigned no reason for that opinion.

(*d*) In *Daubigny* v. *Duval*, 5 T. R. 604.
(*e*) In *Palteney* v. *Keymer*, 3 Esp. 182 (in 1800).
(*f*) *Newsom* v. *Thornton*, 6 East, 17 (in 1805).

the security of the pledge, not to his own purposes, but to the specific object of taking up bills of exchange drawn upon him by his principal against the goods consigned, or of paying the duties, freight, or other charges in connection therewith (*g*). It would seem, however, that the ruling in *Paterson* v. *Tash*, and the series of common law decisions which were based upon its authority, at first attracted but little notice among commercial men. This was doubtless due to the peculiar circumstances of the time. The import trade of Great Britain had been crippled by the long and costly wars in which she was engaged at the close of the last and the opening of the present century, and it was not until after the resumption of peace in 1815, with the rapid growth of commerce and expansion of credit which at once ensued, that the commercial classes awoke to the evils resulting from the existing condition of the law. In 1823 an agitation was set on foot by London merchants, bankers, and brokers, with the view of obtaining an immediate alteration of the law, and petitions were presented to Parliament with that object. A Committee of the House of Commons was appointed to investigate into the law and practice of trade on the subject both at home and abroad; a great number of witnesses were examined, including many of the leading London merchants, and most of the British vice-consuls and commercial representatives on the continent; and the

---

(*g*) *Graham* v. *Dyster* (1817), 6 M. & S. 1. The most important decisions on the factor's power to pledge, after *Paterson* v. *Tash*, and before the passing of the first Factors Act in 1823, are: *Daubigny* v. *Duval*, 5 T. R. 604 (in 1794); *Pulteney* v. *Keymer*, 3 Esp. 182 (in 1800); *M'Combie* v. *Davis*, 7 East, 5 (in 1805); *Newsom* v. *Thornton*, 6 East, 17 (in 1805); *Martini* v. *Coles*, 1 M. & S. 140 (in 1813); *Shiplay* v. *Keymer* ibid. 484 (in 1813); *Solly* v. *Rathbone*, 2 M. & S. 248 (in 1814); *Graham* v. *Dyster*, 6 M. & S. 1 (in 1817); *Boyson* v. *Coles*, ibid. 14 (in 1817); *Barton* v. *Williams*, 5 B. & A. 395 (in 1822).

Committee issued a report strongly urging upon the House the necessity, in the protection of commerce, of an immediate change in the law. This course was strenuously opposed by the legal members of the House, led by Sir James Scarlett (*h*). It is beyond the scope of our present inquiry to discuss the arguments adduced for and against the policy of the change (*i*). We will only remark that from the point of view of commercial expediency the earlier Factors Acts worked a necessary change in the common law. The rule that a factor cannot pledge the goods of his principal was adapted to early times, when merchandise was generally sold in market overt, and the honest purchaser was protected by the rules of the common law, with reference to sales made in market overt. Little credit was then given, and merchants were unable to trade beyond their capital, and seldom required to pledge their stock-in-trade. But the rapid growth of modern commerce has brought with it a vast expansion of credit, and the necessity for fresh facilities in obtaining borrowed capital. Market overt no longer affords adequate protection, because little of the merchandise that is now brought to sale is sold in market overt, and it seems just that the purchaser or pledgee should have the same protection against the owner who permits another to deal with his property as if it were his own, as was afforded him by market overt (*k*). Bankers and brokers are called upon to make advances upon the security of goods or of documents of title, which

---

(*h*) Parliamentary Papers, Vol. IV. for the year 1823; Hansard's Debates, Vol. IX. 211, 256.

(*i*) The arguments are summarised in a note to the case of *Blandy* v. *Allan*, in Danson & Lloyd's Reports, pp. 29 *et seq.*

(*k*) The Legislature, however, as will appear in the sequel, has never extended the principle of "ostensible ownership" to this point, although each of the Factors Acts marks an advance in this direction.

are taken as representing goods, under circumstances which may often render it very difficult, if not impossible, for them to satisfy themselves beforehand that the customer is the real owner of the securities he offers; and the difficulty is increased by the fact that factors are accustomed to carry on business as merchants on their own account. Further, although the old common law rule no doubt protected the foreign consignor or owner against fraudulent dealings by his factor, against which the home-merchant is doubtless in a better position to protect himself, it may be fairly argued, on the other side, that the change of law involved in the Factors Acts conferred an actual benefit on the foreign principal, by enabling his factor to pledge the goods for advances wherewith to meet the principal's drafts, and so save him from a forced sale of the goods, when the market was unfavourable (*l*).

Let us now pass from considerations of policy to those of law. The rule in *Paterson* v. *Tash* was supported, on legal grounds, as being only a particular application of the doctrine of the English common law, that one person can give to another no better title to goods than he himself possesses. This rule was apparently framed upon that of the civil law—*nemo plus juris ad alium transferre potest quam ipse haberet* (*m*)—which we find engrafted on most of the old legal codes of Europe existing before the Code Napoléon (*n*). But the rule was not an inflexible one, and yielded to exceptions, the best known of which

---

(*l*) The arguments in favour of the change are clearly put by Best, C. J., in *Williams* v. *Barton*, 3 Bing. 145, from whose judgment the foregoing observations are mainly taken.

(*m*) The Digest absolutely prohibits pledging by an agent. Cod. lib. 8, tit. 16 ; Dig. lib. 20, tit. 3.

(*n*) All the old text writers in Holland and the maritime states of Italy adopt the rule of the civil law. And the same rule was adopted in France, in Scotland, and in America. The authorities are given in Bell's Commentaries on the Law of Scotland, Vol. I. p. 520.

is a sale in market overt. It also gave place to other considerations arising out of the relationship of principal and agent, and the nature of the particular authority conferred upon the person who is in possession of the property. We refer to the doctrine of estoppel, or "holding out," by which when a person authorizes another to assume the apparent right of disposing of property *in the usual course of his employment*, it is presumed that the apparent authority is real, and the owner is estopped from asserting the contrary. But the implied authority extending only to the usual course of employment, as soon as it was decided that a pledge was beyond the scope of the factor's employment, the case of a pledge fell outside the exception and under the general rule above stated. When we turn from England to foreign countries, we find that the rule laid down in *Paterson* v. *Tash* was contrary to the law and policy of all the other commercial nations of Europe. Although, as we have already said, they originally adopted the rule of the civil law, they afterwards, in the interests of commerce, replaced it in their codes by the doctrine that "possession constitutes title"— that possession is proof of property. And the Committee of the House of Commons reported that this doctrine was the "law of France, Portugal, Spain, Sardinia, Italy, Austria, Holland, the Hanse Towns, Prussia, Denmark, Sweden, and Russia" (and they might have added Scotland (*o*)), and they strongly urged upon Parliament its adoption in this country. The Legislature, therefore, in determining to alter the law, had two courses open to it: either to recognize the doctrine that "possession constitutes title" to the full extent to which it was recognized on the Continent, by conferring a good title in every

---

(*o*) See Bell's Commentaries, Vol. I. p. 517 (7th ed.). The provisions of the French and German codes will be found in Appendix No. 1, *post*, p. 73.

case upon innocent persons dealing with *persons* in the apparent ownership of goods as if they were the real owners, or, by an extension of the doctrine of estoppel, to limit the protection to the particular case of innocent persons dealing with *mercantile agents* under similar circumstances. The Legislature adopted the latter course, but in a very tentative and cautious spirit, owing, we may presume, to the legal opposition raised in the House, and the immediate result was the first Factors Act (4 Geo. IV. c. 83).

This Act went a very little way. It altered the law as to pledging only in the particular case of consignments by sea. Under its provisions a consignee might acquire a lien upon the goods consigned to him for advances made, or securities given, to the consignor, and transfer the lien by a pledge of the goods, or of the bill of lading. It thus repealed the common law rule that a pledge was so wholly tortious as not even to transfer the pledgor's lien. But the consignee must have had no notice that the consignor was not the actual owner. The Act fell far short of the protection required, and was speedily followed by the Factors Act, 1825 (6 Geo. IV. c. 94), the object of which, as stated in the preamble, was to alter and amend the earlier statute, and to make further provisions in relation to the contracts and agreements therein mentioned. The following is a brief summary of the provisions of the Act.

After confirming the protection given by the earlier Act to consignees (*p*), it proceeded to extend the doctrine of estoppel, so as to give validity to a pledge made by a factor who was clothed with ostensible ownership of goods, by being "entrusted with and in possession of" a

---

(*p*) No case has ever arisen requiring a court of law to construe the provisions relating to consignees, probably because they have been found to work harmoniously with the practice of merchants. See per Lord Blackburn in *Mildred* v. *Maspons*, 8 App. Cas. 885.

"document of title" to goods, as specified by the Act, the pledge being made as security either for an advance or in respect of a pre-existing debt, and, in the latter case, being valid to the extent only of the factor's lien upon the goods then enforceable; or, in other words, effectual only to transfer the factor's lien to the pledgee. But what is important to observe is, that so far, the Act required that the pledgee should be ignorant of the factor's real character; so that its effect was not to repeal the "rule in *Paterson v. Tash,*" and to confer directly upon a factor the right to pledge, but only to protect such persons as dealt with an agent clothed with the ostensible ownership of goods on the assumption that he was the real owner. But then the Act went a step forward, and provided that even when the pledgee knew that the person he was dealing with was a factor, the pledge should have the same effect as in the case of a pledge made in respect of an antecedent debt— viz., to transfer the factor's lien to the pledgee—and to this extent only it trenched upon the rule laid down in *Paterson v. Tash.* The Act dealt also with the sale of goods by a factor, but on this point only confirmed the common law, as laid down in several then recent decisions, to the effect that for a sale to be valid by the application of the principle of estoppel, the agent who was clothed with the ostensible ownership of the goods must be one who has an implied authority to sell, either in fact or from the nature and scope of his employment, and the purchaser must have no notice of the agent's want of authority to sell (*q*). These decisions were, doubtless, present to the minds of those who framed the Act; and the fact of the statutory law being confirmatory of the common law on this point is important, as indicating the intention of the Legislature not

---

(*q*) *Wilkinson* v. *King*, 2 Camp. 335 (in 1809); *Pickering* v. *Busk*, 15 East, 38 (in 1812); *Dyer* v. *Pearson*, 3 B. & C. 38 (in 1824).

to extend the doctrine of estoppel, upon which, as we have already remarked, the provisions of the Factors Acts were based, beyond the particular class of factors or agents for sale. The Legislature, unfortunately, failed to express this intention in clear and consistent language. The class of agents whom the Acts were intended to protect were described in the Factors Act, 1823, as "persons intrusted for the purpose of sale"; in the Factors Act, 1825, as "persons intrusted for the purpose of consignment or of sale," "persons intrusted and in possession," "agents intrusted," "factors or agents"; and in the Factors Act, 1842, as "agents intrusted with the possession," and "agents intrusted and possessed." Hence a very large share of the litigation under the Factors Acts arose from endeavours to extend the operation of the Acts either to other classes of agents, who were intrusted with the possession of goods, or of a document of title to goods, but who were not agents for sale, as, *e.g.*, wharfingers, warehousemen, carriers, forwarding agents, and the like; or to persons who were not in any sense agents—*e.g.*, buyers and sellers allowed to obtain or to remain in possession of documents of title to goods sold. These endeavours, however, were all unsuccessful, because the judges in every case construed the intention of the Legislature, however imperfectly expressed, as strictly applying—in spite of the general expressions to be found here and there throughout the Acts— to the particular case of a factor or agent to whose employment a power of sale was ordinarily incident; and the Legislature manifested its acquiescence in this judicial interpretation of the scope of the Acts, by not framing its enactments so as to avoid the effect of these decisions (as it had avoided the effect of others), except in the particular case of a buyer or seller allowed to remain in possession of the documents of title to goods sold, to which the principle of estoppel was expressly extended by the Factors Act, 1877. Reverting to the Factors Act of 1825, we remark that it provided for the right of the true owner to redeem his goods from the factor or his trustee in bankruptcy, or the goods or their proceeds from a purchaser or pledgee from the factor, subject to certain conditions. It also contained penal clauses dealing with the case of a factor fraudulently pledging the goods of his principal, which have since been superseded by the provisions of the Larceny Act (*q*).

The law remained on this footing until the year 1842. It proved to be altogether insufficient as a protection for merchants, who also found in the stringency with which its provisions were construed by the Courts the greatest difficulty in availing themselves of the benefits which it was intended to confer. The Legislature therefore again interfered, and the Factors Act, 1842 (5 & 6 Vict. c. 39), was passed with the object, as declared in the preamble, of altering and amending the earlier Act, and extending the provisions thereof, and of putting the law on a clear and certain basis. The preamble also states that the object of the Act is to place pledges made by known agents upon the same footing upon which sales made by them were placed by the Factors Act, 1825, which the Act accordingly effects in its first section, thus repealing the rule laid down in *Paterson* v. *Tash* just a century earlier, and acknowledging tardily, but unreservedly, the right of a factor to pledge the goods of his principal. The safety of those dealing with factors was thus assured, and the only condition the Act imposed was that the advances to the factor should be made *bonâ fide* and without notice of the agent's want of authority; the object of the Legislature not being of course to enable a factor to deviate from any special instructions of his principal, when such

(*q*) See Appendix No. 2, *post*.

instructions have been brought to the knowledge of those dealing with him. The Act extended the principle of estoppel to the case of a pledge made by a known agent (*i. e.*, a factor), who is "intrusted with the possession of goods, or of the documents of title relating to them;" thus, by the way, extending to the possession of goods the same protection which the Factors Act, 1825, confined to the possession of a document of title.

And here it becomes necessary to refer to the construction which the Courts placed upon the qualifying words, "agent intrusted," in the earlier Factors Acts. The Courts, as we already have had occasion to observe, decided that the "agent" under the Acts must be one to whose employment a power of sale was ordinarily incident, *i. e.*, a factor, or an agent whose employment corresponded to that of a factor; but they further decided that the agent must have received possession of the goods in his capacity as agent for sale, and either for the specific purpose of sale, or for some object connected with the sale. Possession *per se* was only presumptive evidence of intrustment, and it was open to the owner of the goods to repel the presumption, and prove that there was no intrustment in fact.

A few decisions, selected before and after the passing of the Factors Acts, will serve to illustrate the limiting signification which the Courts attached to the expressions "intrusted" and "intrustment." So early as 1809, Lord Ellenborough, at *nisi prius*, decided that when goods were sent to a wharfinger to be warehoused, and the wharfinger also carried on business as a factor, and sold the goods to a purchaser, who bought them *bonâ fide*, and without notice of the agent's want of authority to sell, the sale was invalid, and the transaction a tortious conversion, under which the purchaser could derive no title (*r*). Soon after

(*r*) *Wilkinson* v. *King*, 2 Camp. 335. These cases are set out and considered in a Treatise on the earlier Factors Acts by the Author and Mr. H. F. Boyd, to which the reader is referred generally.

the passing of the two earlier Factors Acts the Courts held that it was not the intention of the Legislature, by those enactments, to alter the effect of this decision. For, in 1831, in the case of a wharfinger who was also a flour factor, and who received flour from the owner in his capacity of wharfinger, and without any authority to sell, and the defendant had purchased the flour without notice of the seller's want of authority, it was decided that the purchaser was not protected by the Factors Act, 1825, and that the owner could maintain trover against him (s). A further, but unsuccessful, endeavour was made in 1874 to bring the case now under consideration within the operation of the Factors Act, 1842, where the agent carried on business in a twofold character, as a warehouseman and broker, and had received goods in the former capacity, which he afterwards pledged for an advance, but the same decision was given under the later as under the earlier Act (t). But the Courts went further. They decided that the factor must have received possession of the goods not only *quâ* factor, but also for the purpose of sale, or, at any rate, for some purpose connected therewith, whether before or after its completion (u). The Factors Act, 1842, contained a proviso to the effect that an agent in possession should be taken to have been intrusted by the owner *unless the contrary appeared in evidence;* and, as was pointed out by eminent judges like Lord Blackburn and Mr. Justice Willes (x), the effect of this proviso was that possession even by an agent belonging to the class of mer-

(s) *Monk* v. *Whittenbury*, 2 B. & Ad. 484.
(t) *Cole* v. *North Western Bank*, L. R. 10 C. P. 354; affirming S. C., L. R. 9 C. P. 470; and see *City Bank* v. *Barrow*, 5 App. Cas. 664.
(u) *Janberry* v. *Britten*, 5 Scott, 655; 4 Bing. N. C. 442; *Baines* v. *Swainson*, 4 B. & S. 270; *Vickers* v. *Hertz*, L. R. 2 H. L. (Sc.) 113.
(x) In *Cole* v. *North Western Bank*, L. R. 10 C. P. at p. 371; and in *Fuentes* v. *Montis*, L. R. 3 C. P. at p. 281.

cantile agents to which the operation of the Acts was limited, and one whose ordinary business it is to sell goods, only raised a *primâ facie* presumption of intrustment. Hence it resulted that a pledgee, and, apparently, a purchaser from an agent so in possession, ran the risk of the owner being able to prove that the goods had been sent to the factor, not for sale, but to be warehoused or forwarded, or that they were in the factor's possession by way of pledge or of loan. A striking illustration of the hardship and risk entailed upon merchants by this interpretation was given in the case of a person making advances to a factor whose authority had been secretly revoked, it being decided that the revocation of authority put an end to the factor's power to pledge, on the ground that, although in possession, he was no longer intrusted with the goods (*y*). This particular hardship was removed by the Factors Act, 1877, but previous to the passing of the present Factors Act, there was no absolute security for persons dealing with factors who were clothed with the ostensible ownership of goods unless and until they had satisfactory proof both of the capacity in which, and of the purpose for which, the factor had received the goods from his principal. We shall deal hereafter with the effect of the present Factors Act in this connection. We need not pause to further consider the provisions of the Factors Act, 1842; it relaxed the stringency of judicial interpretation in certain cases which had been ruled outside the operation and benefit of the earlier Acts, in particular amending the law with reference to the *bonâ fide* exchange of securities made by a factor, and to the possession by a factor of "derivative" documents of title, subjects to which we shall again refer when we come to consider in

(*y*) *Fuentes* v. *Montis*, L. R. 3 C. P. 268 (in 1868).

detail the corresponding provisions of the present Factors Act.

The statutory law remained in this condition for thirty-five years. In 1877 the Legislature again interfered by an enactment (the 40 & 41 Vict. c. 39), the object of which, as stated in its preamble, was to remove doubts which had arisen with respect to the true meaning of certain provisions of the earlier Factors Acts, and to amend the same, for the better security of persons buying or making advances on goods, or the documents of title to goods, in the usual and ordinary course of mercantile business.

It has been already noticed (*ante*, p. 11) that endeavours were made to bring the case of a seller or of a buyer who was allowed to remain in or to obtain possession of a document of title to goods sold, within the definition of a " person intrusted " under the Factors Acts (*z*). In each case the endeavour was unsuccessful, the Courts adhering to the strict interpretation of the word " person " as " agent," whereas the persons in question affected to deal with the goods not as agents but as owners, and in their own right. The singular anomaly thus existed, as was pointed out by Mr. Benjamin in his Treatise on the Law of Sale (*a*), that if a merchant buying goods and paying the price received a transfer of the document of title, he would be safe if his vendor was *not owner* but only assignor of the warrant, and would not be safe if the vendor was *owner*, because the price might remain unpaid to the assignor of

---

(*z*) As relating to a seller, the case was *Johnson* v. *The Crédit Lyonnais Co.*, 2 C. P. D. 224 (affirmed on appeal, 3 C. P. D. 32), decided in 1877, only a few months before the passing of the Factors Act of that year; and as relating to a buyer, the cases of *Jenkyns* v. *Osborne*, 7 M. & G. 678 (in 1844); and *Van Casteel* v. *Booker*, 2 Ex. 691 (in 1848).

(*a*) Benj. on Sale (4th ed. by the Author and Mr. H. F. Boyd), p. 831.

the warrant. This was the necessary result of the conflicting interpretations put on the dock warrant by the Legislature and the Courts. The chief object of the Factors Act, 1877, was to remove this anomaly.

After amending the law to which we have already referred, with respect to the secret revocation of a factor's authority, the Act proceeds to extend the operation of the earlier Acts, and the principle of estoppel upon which they were based, to the cases in question, by, in effect, enacting that a seller or a buyer in possession of a document of title to goods sold should be able to make as valid a sale or pledge as if he were an "agent" or "person intrusted" by the other within the meaning of the Factors Acts; provided that the purchaser or pledgee had no notice of the previous sale, and the first purchaser's rights thereunder, or of the original vendor's rights, as the case might be.

Further, with the object of reconciling the statutory and common law interpretation of warrants and other documents which have been treated by the Legislature and by merchants as authorizing the holder to transfer the actual possession of the goods which they represent, the Act provided that the negotiation of any "document of title," for the definition of which we must apparently turn to the earlier Acts, to a *bonâ fide* transferee for value (purchaser or pledgee) should have the same effect for defeating the vendor's lien or other rights, as the transfer of a bill of lading had at common law for defeating the right of stoppage *in transitu*. It thus extended to dock warrants, delivery orders, &c., the principle laid down in the great leading case of *Lickbarrow* v. *Mason* (b), as applicable to bills of lading only. As, however, the present Factors Act substantially re-enacts this provision of the Factors

---

(b) 1 Sm. L. C. (ed. 1887) 737.

Act, 1877, we propose to postpone any observations we may have to offer upon this topic, until we come to consider those provisions in detail.

The Factors Act, 1877, marked a fresh stage in the history of legislation for the protection of persons dealing with those who are clothed with the ostensible ownership of property. Strictly speaking, it lay altogether outside the scope of the earlier Factors Acts, because it went beyond the class of commercial agents from which those Acts received their name, and to which their operation was, by the strictness of judicial interpretation, practically confined; but it must not be overlooked that its application reached only to the particular class of persons indicated, *i.e.*, sellers and buyers in possession of a document of title to goods sold. It protected merchants, bankers, and others who *bonâ fide* made advances to or purchased goods from such persons without notice of the circumstances under which they were in possession of the *indicia* of property; it had no application either to classes of agents other than factors or agents in the nature of factors, as, *e.g.*, warehousemen or wharfingers, or to factors or agents for sale who were not "intrusted" and in possession of a document of title for the purpose of sale or some object connected therewith. Judicial decisions had ruled these cases to be outside the operation and benefit of the Factors Acts, and the Factors Act, 1877, did not annul, save in the case of a secret revocation of a factor's authority, the effect of any of those decisions. To this limited extent only had the Legislature thought fit to recognize the doctrine that "possession gives title," a doctrine which, as we have already remarked, prevails among the commercial nations of Europe, and which the committee of the House of Commons appointed in 1823 so strongly urged upon Parliament to adopt in this country.

II.—THE FACTORS ACT, 1889.

Having now reviewed the state of the law previous to the Factors Act, 1889, we propose to consider in detail the provisions of that statute.

The Act is intituled "An Act to *amend* and *consolidate* the Factors Acts." Its object, therefore, is two-fold, viz., in part to alter, and in part to confirm the pre-existing law. The Act does not, like the previous Factors Acts, furnish an aid to its own interpretation by commencing with a preamble setting forth the objects which the Legislature had in view, but leaves us to determine in what particulars and to what extent the law has been amended from a consideration of the actual language employed, wherein some difficulty may arise, from the fact that its phraseology differs from that of the previous Acts, and it is not always clear whether a change of language was intended to effect a change in the law, or was adopted merely with a view to uniformity of expression.

The amending portions of the Act, however, appear to be few, and not very important. Setting aside the substitution of a mercantile agent having a prescribed authority for the "agent intrusted" of the previous Acts (sect. 1, sub-sect. 1), which seems to be a formal, and not a substantial, alteration of the law (*post*, pp. 22 *et seq.*), the amendments, which will be considered in detail under the respective sections of the Act, may be briefly summarized as follows:—

1. An authority to pledge is placed upon the same footing with an authority to sell. (Sect. 1, sub-sect. 1.)

2. A liability may form a good consideration, whether present or past, for a pledge. (Sect. 1, sub-sect. 5, and sect. 4.)
3. The consideration for a sale, pledge, or other disposition under the Act is extended. (Sect. 5.)
4. The proviso previously existing as to notice in the case of a pledge for an antecedent debt is repealed. (Sect. 4.)

The Act itself is divided into four parts, the following being a summary of its clauses:—

PART I.—PRELIMINARY.

Definitions of mercantile agent, possession, goods, documents of title, pledge, and person. (Sect. 1.) pp. 21—36.

PART II.—DISPOSITIONS BY MERCANTILE AGENTS.

Deals with a sale, pledge, or other disposition by a mercantile agent in possession, with the consent of the owner, of goods or of the documents of title to goods (sect. 2, sub-sects. 1, 4): pp. 36—40, 42.

Provides (1) for the secret revocation of the agent's authority (sect. 2, sub-sect. 2); (2) for the agent's possession of a "derivative" document of title (sect. 2 sub-sect. 3); (3) for the effect of a pledge of a document of title (sect. 3): pp. 40—42, 43.

Deals with a pledge made in respect of a pre-existing debt or liability (sect. 4): pp. 43—49.

Defines the consideration necessary for the validity of a disposition of goods made in pursuance of the Act (sect. 5): pp. 49—54.

Deals (1) with the exchange of goods or documents held in pledge (sect. 5); (2) with agreements made through a clerk or other authorized person (sect. 6); (3) with the lien of a consignee (sect. 7): pp. 52—54, 54—56.

PART III.—DISPOSITIONS BY SELLERS OR BUYERS OF GOODS.

Deals (1) with the case of a seller remaining in possession (sect. 8), or of a buyer obtaining possession (sect. 9), of goods or documents, and the effect of the delivery or transfer thereof in pursuance of a sale, pledge, or other disposition; (2) with the effect of a transfer of a document of title on the original seller's lien or right of stoppage *in transitu* (sect. 10) : pp. 56—69.

PART IV.—SUPPLEMENTAL.

Deals with the mode of transferring a document of title (sect. 11) : p. 69.

Saves (1) the criminal and civil liability of an agent acting contrary to his authority (sect. 12, sub-sect. 1) ; (2) the right of the owner of goods to recover or redeem them, or the proceeds of their sale, from the agent or his trustee in bankruptcy, or from a pledgee or purchaser from the agent (sect. 12, sub-sects. 2, 3) ; (3) the common law powers of an agent (sect. 13) : pp. 69—72.

Repeals the four earlier Factors Acts, saving existing rights and liabilities (sect. 14) : p. 72.

Provides for the commencement, extent, and title of the Act. (Sects. 15, 16, 17) : p. 72.

Preliminary.

1. For the purposes of this Act—

(1.) The expression "mercantile agent" shall mean a mercantile agent having in the customary course of his business as such agent authority either to sell goods, or to consign goods for the purpose of sale, or to buy goods, or to raise money on the security of goods.

The Act commences with a definition of the class of agent to which its application (ss. 2—7) is limited. The definition is important, not only as indicating the scope of the Act, but also as effecting an alteration in the law. The first question to present itself in any case arising under the Factors Acts is this: is the person dealing with goods or documents of title in his possession an agent within the meaning and intent of the Factors Acts? This is a question of law which depends for its solution upon the construction to be put upon the language of the Acts. Now, as we have already shown, the earlier Factors Acts contained no definition whatever of the particular class of persons to which they were intended to apply. There was no uniformity in the description given by the different Acts, nor even in different clauses of the same Act. Sometimes the class was limited to "agents intrusted," sometimes more widely described as "persons intrusted." Thus we find the following (among other expressions), "a person intrusted for the purpose of sale," "a person intrusted with and in possession," "an agent intrusted," "a factor or agent." The Courts, however, refused to adopt the wider signification which, it was contended, attached to some as compared with others of these expressions. They construed the more general expressions with reference to the general scope and object of the Acts as well as to the particular language used, so as to limit their operation to one and the same class of persons throughout all the Factors Acts, viz., a factor or agent in the nature of a factor, intrusted with the possession of goods as such factor or agent, that is, for the purpose of sale, or for some object connected with the sale (*a*). The agent, therefore, must have received authority from his principal, express or implied, to sell the goods, that is to say, he must either have been intrusted with the goods for the purpose of sale, or have been a person who is ordinarily intrusted to sell such goods, and have made the sale or pledge in the ordinary course of his business, in pursuance of the authority so conferred upon him. The language of the present Act is altered. It no longer requires the agent to be "intrusted," but substitutes for "the agent intrusted" of the previous Acts, a mercantile agent having, in the customary course of

---

(*a*) These last words are inserted to include the decision in *Baines* v. *Swainson*, 4 B. & S. 270.

his business (*b*) as such agent, authority to deal with goods in one or other of the following ways :

(1) To sell goods ;
(2) To consign goods for the purpose of sale ;
(3) To buy goods ;
(4) To raise money on the security of goods.

We have therefore to determine whether the Act by this change of language has effected any corresponding change in the law. What was the object and effect of the previous Factors Acts? The Legislature did not intend by those statutes to provide a remedy for those hardships which accrued to innocent persons by dealing with *persons* in the apparent ownership of goods as if they were the real owners, but only to protect such persons in their dealings with *agents of the owners* of goods—agents "intrusted and in possession." The authority therefore given by the Factors Acts *quoad* third persons was an authority superadded and accessory to the ordinary authority given by a principal to his factor (*c*). The Factors Acts required that the relation of principal and agent should exist between the owner of the goods and the person in possession of them. They also required that the agent should be "intrusted" with the goods, and "intrustment," owing to the judicial construction put upon that word, meant something more than mere possession with the owner's privity and consent. An agent was held to be "intrusted" only when he had received possession of goods or documents of title, *quâ* agent—that is to say, in his capacity as agent for sale, or for some purpose in connection with the sale. And the Factors Act, 1842, contained a very important provision, the effect of which, as expounded by very eminent judges (*d*), was to make

---

(*b*) An agent whose ordinary business was not to sell, but who was authorized to sell in the particular instance, was held to be an "agent intrusted" within the meaning of the previous Act, on the ground that his employment corresponded to that of a factor *pro hâc vice*, and that it was immaterial that it was an isolated instance of his employment: *Heyman* v. *Flewker*, 13 C. B. N. S. 519.

(*c*) See per Willes, J., in *Fuentes* v. *Montis*, L. R. 3 C. P. at p. 282 ; affirming the *dictum* of Blackburn, J., in *Baines* v. *Swainson*, 4 B. & S. 270.

(*d*) Lord Blackburn in *Baines* v. *Swainson*, *ubi supra* ; and Willes, J., in *Fuentes* v. *Montis*, *ubi supra*.

possession of the goods even by a mercantile agent, whose ordinary business it is to sell, only *primâ facie* evidence of intrustment, leaving it open to the owner to rebut that presumption by showing the real nature of the transaction between him and his agent. Thus, to take the case of an agent whose general business it is to sell, being intrusted with goods for a purpose other than that of sale, as, *e.g.*, upon a pledge for an advance with instructions not to sell, or upon loan; or, if he happens to carry on business as a warehouseman as well as a factor, and goods are placed in his possession to be warehoused; in both these cases the agent would, *primâ facie*, be in a position to deal with these goods as factor, and yet, owing to the effect of the proviso to which we have referred, the principal might repel the presumption of the agent's enlarged authority under the Factors Acts, and the persons dealing with the agent would lose the protection of those statutes.

Let us now turn to the clause of the present Act now under consideration. First of all, the Act applies only to agents (*d*). The scope of the Act is not wider than that of the previous Acts. The person who is to give a title as against the owner of the goods must be an agent. If he has no right to the possession of the goods as agent, the provisions of the Act do not apply to him.

Secondly, the agent must be a mercantile agent—that is to say, an agent in a mercantile transaction (*e*).

Thirdly, the mercantile agent must have been authorized by his principal to deal with the goods in his possession in one of the ways specified. In this respect, again, the scope of the Act is not wider than the previous Acts, and the statutory powers which it confers are superadded to the authority conferred upon the agent by his principal, and to the powers resulting therefrom, which the agent can exercise at common law (*f*). But the Act does go beyond the previous Factors Acts in extending the nature of the authority which the agent must

(*d*) Sellers and buyers of goods remaining in possession thereof are treated as agents for the purposes of the Act.

(*e*) Decided under the previous Factors Acts in *Wood* v. *Rowcliffe*, 6 Hare, 183.

(*f*) *Vide* the 13th section of the Act, *post*, p. 71.

possess before he can be invested with the statutory authority. The earlier Acts required, as we have seen, that the agent should have authority to sell, either express or implied. The present Act provides that the agent should be authorized *either* to sell, and that expressly or impliedly (as in the case of a consignor for the purpose of sale, or of a broker or agent to buy goods, having possession of the goods bought), *or* to raise money on the security of goods—*i.e.*, to pledge—thus placing an authority to pledge upon the same footing with an authority to sell. The agent's authority may be expressly conferred by the instructions of his principal, or may be implied from the course of former dealings between the same parties, or from the nature and scope of the agent's business. Thus, a factor, or broker when in possession of goods, has implied authority to sell or pledge them, because the making of contracts for the sale or purchase of goods, or the pledge of them (since 1842), is within the scope of the usual employment of a factor or broker. So, again, a consignor for the purpose of sale, or a consignee for sale, or a broker employed for the purchase of goods, who is allowed to obtain possession of the goods bought—a case to which we shall presently refer—has each implied authority to sell or pledge the goods consigned to him or intrusted to his possession. The important question is as to the right of the owner of the goods to rebut the presumption of authority which arises from the ordinary scope of the agent's employment, by proof of the actual authority given, and to show that the agent was not in fact authorized to deal with the goods in any of the ways specified by this section of the Act. This right was, as we have stated, expressly reserved to the owner by the 4th section of the Factors Act, 1842, and the object of the present section is to preserve the effect of that provision, and of the judicial construction of the word "intrusted" under the previous Acts, by requiring that a mercantile agent, to be within the meaning of the Act, must have such an authority from his principal to deal with goods as is prescribed by the section. We conclude, therefore, that the present Act has not, by its change of language, effected any change in the law. The agent, although no longer "intrusted" in name, must still be "intrusted" in fact, because the Act requires that he should not only be in possession with the owner's privity and consent, but also in possession as a mercantile agent having in the customary course of his business as such agent, authority to sell or pledge the goods of which he is in possession, which corresponds, with the extension of authority to which we have already referred, to the "agent intrusted" of the earlier Acts. It follows that mere possession of goods, or of documents of title by a mercantile agent, even with the owner's consent, will still, as heretofore, only create a presumption of authority to dispose of the goods, which presumption the owner may rebut by proof of the agent not being an agent within the meaning of this section of the Act—that is to say, by proof that the actual authority given was different from the authority prescribed, and that the agent received possession of goods not for the purpose of selling or pledging them, but for some other purpose. If this view of the object and effect of this section be correct, the Act has not altered the old law as laid down in *Wilkinson* v. *King*, *Monk* v. *Whittenbury*, and *Cole* v. *The North Western Bank*, cases to which we have already referred *ante*, p. 13, where the agent carries on business in a twofold character, *e. g.*, as factor or commission agent, and as warehouseman or wharfinger, and having received possession of goods from the owner in his latter capacity, sells or pledges them in his former capacity as an agent for sale. It was decided in these cases that the agent could not confer a good title upon a purchaser or pledgee either at common law or under the previous Factors Acts, which had not altered the law in this respect, the *ratio decidendi* of the cases arising under the Factors Acts being, that the agent must have been "intrusted" with the goods as agent for sale, that is to say, must have received possession of them in that capacity, and for the purpose of sale. Now the warehouseman or wharfinger, who also carries on business as a factor, and who has received possession of goods for the purpose of being warehoused, is not a mercantile agent within the meaning of the Act, since he has not authority as such warehouseman or wharfinger to sell or pledge the goods, and by selling or pledging them in the course of his business as factor, can confer no title upon a purchaser or pledgee. It is, therefore, still necessary for the complete security of persons dealing with mercantile agents, that they should inquire in what capacity, and for what purpose, the agent received possession of goods, for if the agent happens to carry on business in a twofold character, and has received possession of the goods in a capacity which gives him no authority to sell or pledge them, or has received goods, not for the purpose of selling or pledging them, but as bailee by way of loan, or for the purpose of storing or forwarding them, a sale or pledge of the goods by the agent will not be protected by the Factors Act.

Mercantile agents are divided into two principal classes (*y*),

(*g*) Mr. Justice Story enumerates six principal classes of mercantile agents as well-known in commerce, and recognized in Courts of Justice. They are auctioneers, factors, brokers, ship's-husbands, masters of ships, and partners. An auctioneer comes within the statutory definition of a mercantile agent, having, in the customary course of his business as such agent, authority to sell goods; but it is conceived that the provisions of the Factors Act will not apply in his case. A pledge by an auctioneer would be invalidated by reason of the proviso as to notice of the agent's want of authority (sect. 2, sub-sect. 1). Moreover, an auctioneer is a special agent, authorized to sell particular goods in a prescribed mode, viz., by public auction or sale, and the Factors Act is intended to apply to the class of general agents who are authorized to do all acts connected with a particular trade or business. It is sufficient to say of ship's-husbands, and masters of ships, that they have not, under ordinary circumstances, authority to sell or pledge the cargoes of which they have the control. In case of extreme necessity the character of supercargo may be forced upon the ship's-master, or he may, possibly, be appointed by the owner supercargo, or consignee of the cargo. As supercargo, he is a *quasi*-factor who accompanies the cargo which he is employed to sell, but his acts as supercargo must then be treated as distinct from his acts as master, and as though he acted as a different person in each capacity. An interesting question may arise, whether a partner comes within the operation of the Act. Every partner is, in contemplation of law, the general and accredited agent of the partnership, and if the partnership is a commercial one, each partner has implied authority to sell or pledge the property of the firm. A partner, therefore, seems to fall within the definition of a "mercantile agent," as given by the Act. The question was never raised under the earlier Factors' Acts. Lord Justice Lindley, (Treatise on Partnership, p. 140, ed. 1888,) is of opinion that those Acts

namely, factors who are intrusted with the possession as well as the disposal of property, and brokers who are employed to contract only, without being put into possession (*h*). We believe that among merchants the term "broker" is used generally of both classes of agents, and that the term "factor" is not in use except with a limited signification in certain special trades, *e. g.*, corn-factors and coal-factors (*i*).

A factor has been defined to be an agent employed to sell goods or merchandise consigned or delivered to him by or for his principal for a compensation commonly called factorage or commission (*k*), or more briefly as "an agent intrusted with the possession of goods for the purpose of sale" (*l*).

A factor has implied authority:—

1. To sell goods in his own name, and upon reasonable credit (*m*).
2. To receive payment of the price either in cash or by cheque (*n*).
3. To sell at such time and at such price as he may think best (*o*).
4. To warrant goods if that is the custom of the trade (*p*).
5. To insure goods (*q*).
6. To pledge goods (as conferred upon him by the Factors Act, 1842).

neither extended nor abridged the common law powers of a partner to sell or pledge the goods of the firm. They did not render valid any sale or pledge by a partner of partnership goods which was not valid independently of the Acts, on the principles of the common law. It is believed that the present Act will not be found to have any greater effect than the earlier legislation in extending a partner's common law powers, and it expressly provides, by the thirteenth section, that it shall not have any effect in abridging them.

(*h*) Smith's Mercantile Law (9th ed.), p. 106.

(*i*) It is curious to note that, except in the titles of the Acts, the word "factor" occurs only once throughout the series of Factors Acts, namely, in sect. 5 of the Factors Act, 1825.

(*k*) Story on Agency, § 33; Com. Dig. Merchant, B.

(*l*) Per Cotton, L. J., in *Stevens* v. *Biller*, 25 Ch. D. at p. 37.

(*m*) *Ex parte Dixon*, 4 Ch. D. 133; *Scott* v. *Surnam*, Willes, 400, 406.

(*n*) *Drinkwater* v. *Goodwin*, Cowp. 251.

(*o*) *Smart* v. *Sanders*, 3 C. & B. 380.

(*p*) *Pickering* v. *Busk*, 15 East, 38, 45.

(*q*) *Lucena* v. *Crawford*, 2 B. & P. N. R. 269, per Lord Eldon.

A factor is often termed a *commission agent*, or *consignee for sale*, and the goods delivered to him for sale are called a *consignment*. A factor may also be the *consignor* of the goods, including under that term both the foreign merchant shipping goods to this country for sale, or the home agent forwarding goods from a distance for that purpose, and the consignee here to whom goods are shipped or forwarded, not for sale, but for the purpose of re-consignment for sale abroad. In these cases the factor answers the statutory definition of a mercantile agent, having authority to consign goods for the purpose of sale.

A broker may be defined to be an agent employed among merchants and others to make contracts between them, in matters of trade, commerce and navigation for a commission, commonly called brokerage (*r*). Brokers, as distinguished from factors, are not ordinarily intrusted with the possession and control of the goods which they are employed to sell or to buy; so that the provisions of the Factors Act (ss. 2—7), which relate only to mercantile agents in possession of goods or of documents of title to goods, will not apply to them. But in practical business the character of broker and factor is often combined; brokers have possession of the goods they are employed to sell, or are authorized to obtain possession of the goods they are employed to buy. Moreover, brokers are often capitalists who make advances on goods, and have them transferred into their own names as security. A broker under these circumstances is more than a mere broker, and is strictly a factor, having equally with a factor a lien for his commission.

The statutory definition of mercantile agent will include both brokers who are employed to sell and to buy goods, and the Act will protect dispositions made by them when in possession of goods or of the documents of title relating to the goods which they have been employed to sell or to buy. So far as relates to a broker for the purchase of goods, the Act only confirms what was decided at common law so long ago as 1812, in *Pickering* v. *Busk* (*s*). In that case the plaintiff,

(*r*) See Story on Agency, § 28.
(*s*) 15 East, 38.

the owner of goods, had purchased them through Swallow, who pursued the public business of broker and an agent for sale, and the goods were, at the plaintiff's desire, transferred into Swallow's name. It was held that this proved that Swallow had an implied authority to sell, and consequently that the defendants were justified in buying of him and paying him the price. The case was decided on the ground of an implied authority, in fact, to sell, but Lord Ellenborough went further, and said, "If a person authorizes another to assume the apparent right of disposing of property in the ordinary course of trade (*i. e.*, in intrusting it to an agent whose customary business is to sell), it must be presumed that the apparent authority is the real authority. I cannot subscribe to the doctrine that a broker's engagements are necessarily and in all cases limited to his actual authority, the reality of which is afterwards to be tried by the fact. It is clear that he may bind his principal within the limits of the authority with which he has been apparently clothed by his principal in respect of the subject-matter, and there would be no safety in mercantile matters if he could not." The Factors Act confirms the common law as laid down in *Pickering* v. *Busk*, by providing that a broker who is authorized to sell or to buy goods, shall have, when allowed by the owner to obtain possession of the goods, and so to assume the apparent right of disposing of them, implied authority to dispose of them in the ordinary course of his business.

Lastly, the statutory definition includes a mercantile agent who is authorized in the customary course of his business to raise money on the security of goods. The previous Factors Acts required that the agent should have been intrusted for the purpose of sale, or of some object connected therewith; the present Act extends its operation to the case of a mercantile agent who is authorized to pledge the goods of his principal, and puts an authority to pledge upon the same footing with an authority to sell.

There is a class of brokers who are employed to raise money upon securities which are placed in their possession for that purpose. They act as intermediaries between bankers and others advancing money and borrowers, and are in the habit of lending money to their customers upon the securities which are deposited with them, and which they then pledge with the bankers who advance them the money. Independently of the Factors Act, brokers can make a valid pledge of securities, such as bills of exchange or promissory notes, which are negotiable at common law, and of instruments which are negotiable by the custom of trade, such as bonds payable to bearer, and bankers are perfectly safe in dealing with them, provided they make the advances in good faith and without notice of the broker's want of authority (*t*).

The effect of the Act appears to be to extend the same protection to sales and "other dispositions" made by factors and brokers in possession of goods or of documents of title to goods, for the purpose of pledging them, which the previous Factors Acts gave to pledges made by those agents when "intrusted" with goods or documents of title for the purpose of sale.

The following kinds of agents who, owing to the effect of judicial decisions, were excluded from the operation of the previous Factors Acts, are, under the statutory definition now given of a mercantile agent, equally excluded from the operation of the present Act :—

 (1.) Agents who have the control or management of goods only, as *e. g.*, clerks or servants, cashiers, caretakers and the like (*u*).

 (2.) Agents with whom goods are deposited for safe custody, as *e. g.*, bailees, wharfingers and warehousemen (*x*).

 (3.) Agents who are employed in the carriage of goods, as *e. g.*, carriers or forwarding agents (*y*).

 (2.) A person shall be deemed to be in possession of goods, or of the documents of title to goods, where the goods or documents are in his actual custody, or

---

(*t*) *Goodwin* v. *Roberts*, 1 App. Cas. 476 ; *Lord Sheffield's Case, Easton* v. *London Joint Stock Bank*, 13 App. Cas. 333.

(*u*) *Lamb* v. *Attenborough*, 1 B. & S. 831.

(*x*) *Monk* v. *Whittenbury*, 2 B. & Ad. 484.

(*y*) *Hellings* v. *Russell*, 33 L. T. N. S. 380 ; and see *City Bank* v. *Barrow*, 5 App. Cas. 664, 674.

are held by any other person subject to his control or on his behalf.

This re-enacts a provision contained in the 4th section of the Factors Act, 1842. It enables a mercantile agent, who has pledged goods for less than their value, to effect a further pledge of the same goods for the surplus value remaining after satisfying the first pledgee's claim; being the extent to which the first pledgee holds the goods subject to the agent's control and on his behalf (*b*).

(3.) The expression "goods" shall include wares and merchandize.

"Goods, wares and merchandize," comprehend all corporeal moveable property, but not shares, stocks, choses in action, and other incorporeal rights and property (*c*). The expression "goods" will, it is conceived, not only include wares and merchandize, but will be restricted to the class of goods coming under that description, *viz.*, goods in a mercantile sense. The Act contemplates only mercantile transactions; the agent must be a mercantile agent, and the goods of which he is in possession, merchandize (*d*).

(4.) The expression "document of title" shall include any bill of lading, dock warrant, warehouse-keeper's certificate, and warrant or order for the delivery of goods, and any other document used in the ordinary course of business as proof of the possession or control of goods, or authorizing or purporting to authorize, either by endorsement or by delivery, the possessor of the document to transfer or receive goods thereby represented:

This definition corresponds with the one given in the

(*b*) *Portalis* v. *Tetley*, 5 Eq. 140.

(*c*) Stock certificates were held not to be "goods" within the meaning of the earlier Factors Acts: *Freeman* v. *Appleyard*, 32 L. J. Ex. 175.

(*d*) It was held, under the Factors Act, 1842, that "goods" must have this limited sense, and did not include furniture in a furnished house: *Wood* v. *Rowcliffe*, 6 Hare, 191.

4th section of the Factors Act, 1842, only omitting "India warrants," a class of documents which are no longer in use (*f*).

Documents of title are, strictly speaking, documents the title represented by which is derived from the instrument itself, and not from the title of the person from whom the holder received it. But at common law it was necessary that the transferor of a bill of lading should either himself have a title to the goods represented, or be authorized to act for one who had, and it is presumed that the transfer of a warrant or delivery order had certainly no greater effect in passing property than that of a bill of lading. We shall find, when we come to consider the effect of a transfer of one of the documents under the 10th section, that the Act has not rendered them negotiable, as a bill of exchange is negotiable, but has estopped the owner of goods who has issued such a document from setting up a title as against the possessor thereof. Independently of the Factors Acts, the Courts have always declined to treat dock warrants, delivery orders, and warehouse warrants or certificates as being documents of title. The judicial interpretation of them has been that they are mere "offers" or "tokens of authority" to receive possession of goods, inchoate and incomplete until the assignee has obtained the assent of the warehouseman or other custodian of the goods to attorn to him. On the other hand, the practice of merchants as repeatedly attested by special juries, is to treat these documents (*g*) as transferring by indorsement the actual possession of the goods which they represent. Thus, in *Lucas* v. *Dorrien* (*h*), Dallas, C. J., said, in reference to a dock warrant, "I have been several times stopped by a special jury, they being satisfied that the goods pass from hand to hand by the indorsement of these instruments. All special juries cry out with one voice that the

---

(*f*) Cf. also the definition given in the 78th section of the Larceny Act, 1861 (*vide* Appendix); and the definition of "delivery orders" and "warrants" in the Stamp Act, 1870.

(*g*) Certainly dock warrants and certificates, but the practice as to delivery orders is not so clearly established.

(*h*) 7 Taunt. 278.

practice is that the produce lodged in the docks is transferred by indorsing over the certificates and dock-warrants." Further, the Legislature based many enactments (the Factors Acts, Legal Quays Act, and Sufferance Wharves Act) upon the assumption that these documents are used in the ordinary course of business "as proof of the possession or control of goods," or "authorizing the possessor to transfer goods represented thereby"(*i*). And the Factors Act, 1877, gave to the transfer of one of these instruments from a vendee to a sub-vendee or pledgee the same effect as the transfer of a bill of lading already had at common law.

The important part of the definition is its concluding clause. The question whether any particular document, as, *e.g.*, a wharfinger's certificate (which is expressly included as a "document of title" in the Factors Act, 1825) comes within the general words of the definition, must depend upon whether the issuer of the document has represented therein that the goods to which it refers are free from any vendor's lien. If the document contains such a representation, the person issuing it is estopped from setting up his claim as unpaid vendor to the goods as against a *bonâ fide* holder of the document. Thus, when a wharfinger's certificate is in the form of a delivery warrant, making the goods deliverable to "A. B. or his assigns by indorsement or otherwise," the certificate represents the goods and is used as proof of the possession or control of them; it is, therefore, equivalent to a "document of title." If, on the other hand, the certificate only states that the goods are ready for delivery, it is not intended to represent the goods nor to entitle the holder to possession of them; it is, therefore, not equivalent to a "document of title," and no alleged custom of trade can give it the effect of one (*k*).

(*i*) See Mr. Benjamin's remarks on the subject: Benjamin on Sale (4th ed.), p. 829.

(*k*) Recent cases upon the construction of trade documents, alleged to be "documents of title," are: *Gunn* v. *Bolckow, Vaughan & Co.* (1875), 16 Ch. 491 (wharfinger's certificate); *Farmeloe* v. *Bain* (1876), 1 C. P. D. 445 ("undertakings" to deliver); *Merchant Banking Co.* v. *Phœnix Bessemer Steel Co.* (1877), 5 Ch. D. 205 (iron warrants).

(5.) A pledge shall include any contract pledging or giving a lien or security on goods, whether in consideration of an original advance, or of any further or continuing advance, or of any pecuniary liability.

Under the first section of the Factors Act, 1842, which contained the pre-existing law with relation to pledges, the only valid consideration for a pledge was an actual money advance made by the pledgee to the agent, or to some third person at the agent's request. By the words " or of any pecuniary liability " (which were added to the Bill in the Standing Committee on Trade), the Legislature has extended the consideration so as to include any pecuniary liability incurred by the pledgee on the agent's behalf. It is presumed that by a pecuniary liability is meant a liability to pay money, whether *in præsenti* or *in futuro*, and not a liability accrued due (*i.e.*, a debt arising from a liability), as distinguished from an accruing liability. Thus, *e.g.*, a liability in respect of bills accepted by the pledgee on the agent's account, which may or may not ripen into an actual debt, or a liability incurred under a guarantee, or as surety, would be a valid consideration for a pledge.

We shall have occasion to refer to this point again in connection with the power conferred under the fourth section of the Act upon the agent to pledge in respect of a pre-existing liability as well as a pre-existing debt (*post*, pp. 47 *et seq.*).

The provisions of the Factors Act, 1842, were framed entirely with reference to the case of an actual money payment being made to the agent by the pledgee; but as the joint effect of this and the 5th section of the present Act, the consideration for a pledge may now be either an advance made to the person or a pecuniary liability incurred on his behalf, or the transfer to him of other goods or of a document of title, or " any other valuable consideration," the effect of which we shall consider in dealing with the fifth section.

We may remark that the " further or continuing advance " need not necessarily be made to the same person to whom the original advance was made, but may be made to a third person at the agent's request (*m*).

(6.) The expression " person" shall include any body of persons, corporate or unincorporate.

See now sect. 19 of the Interpretation Act, 1889.

Dispositions by Mercantile Agents.

2.—(1.) Where a mercantile agent is, with the consent of the owner, in possession of goods or of the documents of title to goods, any sale, pledge, or other disposition of the goods, made by him when acting in the ordinary course of business of a mercantile agent, shall, subject to the provisions of this Act, be as valid as if he were expressly authorized by the owner of the goods to make the same; provided that the person taking under the disposition acts in good faith, and has not at the time of the disposition notice that the person making the disposition has not authority to make the same.

This second section of the Act in effect provides that a mercantile agent who is, with the consent of the owner, in possession of goods, or of the documents of title to goods, shall have implied authority to make a sale, pledge, or other disposition of the goods, provided (1) that he is acting in the ordinary course of business of a mercantile agent; (2) that the person taking under the disposition acts in good faith, and without notice of the agent's want of authority.

Turning to the corresponding provision of the earlier Factors Acts, we find that they in effect provided that an agent *intrusted* with and in possession of goods, or of the documents of title to goods, should have implied authority to make

(*m*) *Sheppard* v. *The Union Bank of London*, 7 H. & N. 661, overruling the contrary opinion of Wood, V.-C., in *Portalis* v. *Tetley*, 5 Eq. at p. 146.

a valid sale or pledge of the goods, provided (1) that the disposition was made in the ordinary course of business, and (2) that the purchaser or pledgee had no notice that the agent was acting *malâ fide*, or without authority (*n*).

The present Act substantially confirms the law as contained in the previous Factors Acts, and interpreted by judicial decisions. For the "agent intrusted and in possession" of the previous Acts, it substitutes a mercantile agent in possession with the owner's consent, that is to say, a mercantile agent as previously defined, viz., one having authority either to sell goods, or to consign them for sale, or to buy or to pledge goods. But, as we have already stated, this change of language does not seem to effect any change in the law except by placing an authority to pledge upon the same footing with an authority to sell.

With reference to the owner's consent, the Act provides that possession shall be only presumptive evidence of the owner's consent thereto. (Sect. 2, sub-sect. 4.) The Legislature never of course intended to authorize an agent to dispose of his principal's property without his consent, and it accordingly leaves it open to the owner to prove that the agent's possession was obtained without his consent. But the fact that the consent of the owner has been obtained by fraud will not affect the title of a person claiming under a disposition made by the agent, provided that the owner has been induced by the fraudulent representations to give the agent possession of the goods or documents of title, *as his agent*, or, in the language of the previous Factors Acts, has intrusted the agent therewith (*o*). But if an agent obtains mere *possession* of the goods or documents by fraud without being intrusted, *i. e.*, without receiving possession as agent of the owner, or as vendee, then he has no title at all, either as principal or agent, and can convey none to anybody else either at common law or under the Factors Act (*p*). This was

---

(*n*) This is the effect of sects. 2 and 4 of the Act of 1825, and sects. 1 and 2 of the Act of 1842.

(*o*) *Sheppard* v. *Union Bank of London*, 7 H. & N. 66; cf. *Vickers* v. *Hertz*, L. R. 2 H. L. (Sc.) 113; and *Baines* v. *Swainson*, 4 B. & S. 270.

p) *Kingsford* v. *Merry*, 11 Ex. 577; and in Cam. Scacc. 1 H. & N. 503.

the point decided in *Kingsford* v. *Merry* (*p*), a case which created some excitement among city merchants who did not at first understand its true import.

As to "possession," "goods," "documents of title," and "pledge," see the definitions given in the first section, and the notes thereon (*ante*, pp. 31—36).

"Sale, pledge, or other disposition." The Act does not expressly provide for the case of an agent contracting to sell or pledge goods before he has obtained possession of them, and it seems to require, for the validity of a sale or pledge, that the agent should be already in possession of the goods or documents of title. With regard to a sale, if the question arises for decision, it will probably be held, as under the previous Factors Acts, that it is sufficient for the agent to be in possession of goods or documents of title for the purpose of completing a sale which he has already entered into (*q*); but it is more doubtful whether the protection of the Act can be extended to the case of an agent being advised that goods are coming forward to him, and agreeing to pledge them as soon as he gets them, and the bills of lading are in his hands (*r*).

With reference to the "other disposition" referred to in the section. It was held under the Factors Act, 1825, on the meaning of the words "sale or disposition" used in the second section of that Act, that the Legislature, by the introduction of the term "disposition," did not intend to protect any transaction which was essentially distinct from a sale or pledge. And, therefore, when it appeared that the transaction in question was neither in the nature of a sale, nor was such a pledge as was contemplated by the statute, it was held that it did not come within the protection of the Factors Act at all (*s*). But it is not necessary to put this narrow construction upon the language of the present Act, because the fifth section of the Act expressly gives validity to

---

(*p*) 11 Ex. 577; and in Cam. Scacc. 1 H. & N. 503.

(*q*) *Vickers* v. *Hertz*, L. R. 2 H. L. (Sc.) App. 113; *Fuentes* v. *Montis*, L. R. 3 C. P. at p. 279, per Willes, J.

(*r*) This case was possibly provided for in the 4th section of the Factors Act, 1842. See per Wood, V.-C., in *Portalis* v. *Tetley*, 5 Eq. 140.

(*s*) *Taylor* v. *Keymer*, 3 B. & Ad. 320, 337; *Taylor* v. *Trueman*, 1 Moo. & M. 453.

a sale or pledge, the consideration for which is not a pecuniary one, but the delivery or transfer of other goods or documents of title to goods, or in other words empowers a mercantile agent to barter the goods of his principal, which he was prohibited from doing at common law (t). Effect may, therefore, be given to the "other disposition" of the second section by reference to the barter, exchange, or other disposition rendered valid by the fifth section.

"In the ordinary course of business of a mercantile agent." Selling and pledging are assumed to be within the ordinary scope of business of a mercantile agent, and a purchaser or pledgee will not be under the obligation of proving that the sale or pledge was made in the ordinary course of business, although when the facts have been proved it may turn out that the circumstances in which the transaction was carried out were so unusual and out of the course of business as not to bring the transaction within the protection of the Act (u).

The section contains the proviso that "the person taking under the disposition acts in good faith, and has no notice of the agent's want of authority."

It is not the object of the Legislature to authorize an agent to pledge another man's property, or to deviate from the authority he has received from the owner, and its purpose is only to protect *bonâ fide* dispositions. There must be a *bonâ fide* advance made to the agent, or a *bonâ fide* liability incurred on his behalf by the pledgee. If the transaction is only colourably an advance, and is in reality a means of relieving the pledgee from a liability, the transaction will be invalidated. Thus, when the pledgee was liable jointly with a factor on a bill of lading which was overdue, and advanced money to the factor upon the security of goods for the purpose of taking up the bill, the jury were directed that if the transaction was only a circuitous mode of paying the bill upon which the pledgee was liable, it was not protected by the Factors Act, 1825 (v). The question of *bonâ fides* is one for the jury to decide.

(t) *Guerreiro* v. *Peile*, 3 B. & Ald. 616.
(u) Upon this point, see the judgment of Wilde, B., in *Sheppard* v. *Union Bank of London*, 7 H. & N. at p. 673.
(v) *Learoyd* v. *Robinson*, 12 M. & W. 743.

As the present Act, like the previous Factors Acts, is silent as to what will constitute notice, it must be left to the ordinary principles of evidence. The notice may be actual or constructive. Actual notice may be verbal or in writing (since the Act does not stipulate for a written notice). With regard to constructive notice, it was held by Lord Tenterden, in 1830, that notice includes not only a knowledge of the agent's want of authority arising from direct communication, but a knowledge of circumstances, from which a reasonable man of business, applying his understanding to them, would know that such was the case (*x*). This statement has been cited with approval in subsequent decisions, but the modern tendency, no doubt, is to limit the doctrine of constructive notice, and not readily to extend it to honest mercantile transactions. It seems to be doubtful how far knowledge, from whatever source derived, will, as distinguished from notice, affect the validity of the transaction, but it is certain that mere suspicion that the agent is acting without authority will not be sufficient to deprive the person dealing with him of the protection afforded by the statute (*y*).

(2.) **Where a mercantile agent has, with the consent of the owner, been in possession of goods or of the documents of title to goods, any sale, pledge, or other disposition, which would have been valid if the consent had continued, shall be valid notwithstanding the determination of the consent : provided that the person taking under the disposition has not at the time thereof notice that the consent has been determined.**

This sub-section provides for the case of a secret revocation of the agent's authority.

(*x*) *Evans* v. *Trueman*, 1 Moo. & Rob. 10.
(*y*) On the subject of notice, the reader may consult *Evans* v. *Trueman*, *supra* ; *Gobind Chunder Sein* v. *Ryan*, 9 Moo. Ind. App. 140 ; *Navulshaw* v. *Brownrigg*, 2 De G. M. & G. 44 ; *Kaltenbach* v. *Lewis*, 24 Ch. D. 54 (C. A.) ; 10 App. Cas. 617.

Under the Factors Act, 1842, it was held in *Fuentes* v. *Montis* (z), in 1868, that a pledge of goods made by a factor after the revocation of his authority was not protected by the Act, although the person making the advance had no notice of the revocation, the proviso contained in the fourth section of the Factors Act, 1842, enabling the owner of the goods to prove that at the time of the pledge the agent was not in fact "intrusted" with the goods. This decision much shook the confidence felt by merchants, bankers, and others in making advances to factors on the security of goods intrusted to them, for they had no means of ascertaining whether the foreign consignor had or had not revoked the factor's authority. Consequently, in 1877, the Legislature intervened and amended the law on this point, and this sub-section substantially re-enacts the second section of the Factors Act, 1877.

It may be observed that a *sale* made by a factor after the revocation of his authority would be valid independently of this statutory provision, the rule of the common law being that when a principal employs a factor, he will be bound by contracts made by him on his behalf, even after he has revoked the agency, provided that the person dealing with the factor had no notice of the revocation (*a*).

(3.) Where a mercantile agent has obtained possession of any documents of title to goods by reason of his being or having been, with the consent of the owner, in possession of the goods represented thereby, or of any other documents of title to the goods, his possession of the first-mentioned documents shall, for the purposes of this Act, be deemed to be with the consent of the owner.

This sub-section deals with the case of an agent who is in possession of documents of title, which he has been enabled

---

(z) L. R. 3 C. P. 268.
(a) *Trueman* v. *Loder*, 11 A. & E. 589.

to obtain through his possession of goods represented thereby, or of other documents of title, and it enacts that the possession of these first-mentioned documents shall be deemed to be with the owner's consent. Where a mercantile agent receives from the owner possession of goods, or of a bill of lading, by means of which he is enabled to obtain possession of a dock warrant, delivery order, &c., there will be *primâ facie* presumption that the owner consented to his being in possession of these latter documents, and a sale or pledge effected by means of them will be protected by the Act, it being open to the owner, however (under sub-sect. 4, *infra*), to prove that the possession was not with his consent, which he might do by showing that he had expressly prohibited the agent from obtaining the documents.

Under the two earlier Factors Acts of 1823 and of 1825 it was decided that, in the absence of evidence to prove that the possession of the document was necessary for the purpose of sale, the document pledged must have been derived immediately from the owner of the goods, on the ground that to constitute an "intrustment" of the document it was necessary that the owner should have intended the factor to possess it in the particular form in which it was at the time of the pledge, and that intrusting an agent with the document was essentially different from enabling him to become possessed of it (*b*). The Act of 1842 amended the law as laid down in these decisions, and enacted that mere possession of a "derivative" document of title should be *primâ facie* evidence of an "intrustment" of it, and this sub-section substantially re-enacts the provision contained in the first section of the Factors Act, 1842, substituting, as before, "possession with consent" for "intrustment."

(4.) For the purposes of this Act the consent of the owner shall be presumed in the absence of evidence to the contrary.

It is not the object of the Legislature to authorize an agent

---

(*b*) *Phillips* v. *Huth*, 6 M. & W. 572; *Hatfield* v. *Phillips*, 9 M. & W. 672.

to dispose of his principal's property without the principal's consent. Consent will be *prima facie* presumed from the fact of possession, but it will be open to the owner to rebut the presumption by proving that he has not clothed the agent with the apparent authority to deal with his property. Thus, when the agent obtains possession of the goods feloniously, or contrary to or without the authority express or implied of the owner, the Act will not apply. But the owner's consent will be implied from his knowledge of and acquiescence in the agent's possession.

3. A pledge of the documents of title to goods shall be deemed to be a pledge of the goods.

The object of this section, it is believed, is to remove the doubt which has been expressed as to whether the third section of the Factors Act, 1825, which was very inartistically framed, extended to protect a pledge of a document of title to goods made by a factor in respect of a pre-existing debt. Generally, under the earlier Acts, it was provided that a pledge of a document of title should have the same effect as a pledge of the actual goods. (See the second and third sections of the Factors Act, 1825, the first section of the Factors Act, 1842, and the third and fourth sections of the Factors Act, 1877.)

4. Where a mercantile agent pledges goods as security for a debt, or liability due from the pledgor to the pledgee before the time of the pledge, the pledgee shall acquire no further right to the goods than could have been enforced by the pledgor at the time of the pledge.

This section deals with the case of a pledge made by a mercantile agent as security for a pre-existing debt or liability due from him to the pledgee, and it provides that the pledgee shall acquire only the same right to the goods which could have been enforced by the agent at the time of the pledge, or in other words, that the pledge operates only as a transfer of the agent's lien so far as it is enforceable at the time of the pledge, and is a valid security to that extent only.

The case of a pledge made in respect of a pre-existing debt formed the subject-matter of the third section of the Factors Act, 1825 (c), and this section of the present Act, while confirming the old law as to the effect of a pledge for a past consideration, at the same time goes further, and amends the law in two important particulars : (1) in repealing the proviso as to notice of the pledgor's agency contained in the Factors Act, 1825; (2) in extending to an antecedent liability the protection which was previously confined to an antecedent debt.

Under the Factors Act, 1825, a pledge made by a factor in respect of a pre-existing debt was valid only when the pledgee had no notice of the pledgor's agency, and a clause in the third section of the Factors Act, 1842, was inserted apparently with the object of retaining this proviso (d). Under the present Act, the fact that the pledgee has notice that he is dealing with an agent will not affect the validity of the pledge.

Again, while under the Factors Act, 1825, it was required that the pledge should be one in respect of an "antecedent debt *or demand*" (these last words not widening the consideration), the present Act extends its operation to an "antecedent debt *or liability*" due from the pledgor to the pledgee, the effect of which we shall have to consider later on.

The subject-matter of the section may be conveniently treated under the following heads :—(1) The nature of a factor's lien; (2) what constitutes a lien entitling a factor to pledge under this section; and (3) what constitutes an antecedent debt or liability.

(1.) The nature of a factor's lien.

At common law a factor,—and a broker who is in possession of goods about which he is employed has a corresponding

---

(c) It is assumed that the 3rd section of the Factors Act, 1842, had no effect in repealing the 3rd section of the Factors Act, 1825 : *vide Jewan* v. *Whitworth*, 2 Eq. at p. 703.

(d) See Russell on Mercantile Agency (ed. 1873), p. 120.

right,—is entitled to a general lien upon the goods of his principal in his possession *as factor*, not only for all charges and disbursements incurred and paid in relation to the particular goods, but also for the general balance of the account between him and his principal (*e*). This lien entitles him to retain possession of the goods until his claims upon his principal are satisfied. It is deemed to exist in all cases, unless the contrary presumption is clearly established, but it fails when the contrary presumption is clearly established, or *à fortiori*, if an express agreement repelling it is proved (*f*). At common law, the lien, being only the right to retain possession, could not be transferred (*g*); and one effect of the Factors Acts was to abrogate the common law rule so far as relates to pledges made by mercantile agents. It is important to observe that the factor's lien only extends to goods which have come into his possession *as factor*. It follows that if the goods are in the agent's possession as bailee, or wharfinger, or warehouseman, and the agent carries on business at the same time as a factor, he cannot make a valid pledge of the goods under this section, because, having received the goods as bailee, wharfinger, or warehouseman, he has no lien which he can transfer to the pledgee. Again, the factor's right of lien will be defeated when he has obtained possession of the goods by means of false representations, or in a manner not authorized by the principal (*h*). It has been decided that a factor does not lose his right of lien because he has received particular instructions as to the price and the manner of sale (*i*).

(2.) What constitutes a lien entitling the factor to pledge the goods under this section.

The lien under this section must be a right enforceable by the factor at the time of the pledge. Under sect. 5 of the Act of 1825, which was similarly worded, and which may therefore serve as an illustration, although it did not deal with the subject of antecedent debts, it was held that a factor's

---

(*e*) *Kruger* v. *Wilcox*, Amb. 252.
(*f*) Story on Agency, § 378.
(*g*) *Daubigny* v. *Duval*, 5 T. R. 604; *M'Combie* v. *Davies*, 7 East, 6.
(*h*) *Madden* v. *Kempster*, 1 Camp. 12; *Taylor* v. *Robinson*, 8 Taunt. 648.
(*i*) *Stevens* v. *Biller*, 25 Ch. D. 31.

liability under acceptances for his principal did not amount to a lien which he could transfer to a pledgee, because such a liability was not enforceable at the time of the pledge, the right to enforce being interpreted to mean the right to call for the payment of money (*k*). But it is to be observed, that the *ratio decidendi* of *Blandy* v. *Allan* was principally based upon a comparison of the 8th section of the Factors Act, 1825, which provided that the acceptance of bills by a factor should not create a lien so as to protect the factor on a charge of misdemeanor for illegal pledging. But this 8th section was soon after repealed (by 7 & 8 Geo. IV. c. 29, s. 51), and the Larceny Act (*l*), which now embodies the law on this subject, expressly provides (sect. 78) that a factor *may* add to the actual money debt due to him from his principal the amount of any bill of exchange drawn by or on account of his principal. On the assumption that the present section would be interpreted in the light of this provision, it is submitted that a factor's liability under acceptances will now constitute a lien entitling him to pledge under this section (*m*). Even if the factor under acceptances cannot transfer an absolute lien, there seems no reason why he should not be able to transfer the *conditional* lien which he possesses. So long as he is under liability in respect of bills of exchange accepted on his principal's behalf, he is entitled to be indemnified by his principal against such liability, and this is a right which he can enforce against his principal so long as the liability exists. If the principal discharges the liability, the lien is lost, and a pledgee of the goods cannot retain them as against the owner; but until the liability is discharged there seems no reason why the pledgee should not exercise the defeasible lien which the factor was in a position to transfer to him.

Again, it has been held that a mere money claim of the factor against his principal will not constitute a lien entitling the factor to pledge under this section, unless it appears that

---

(*k*) *Fletcher* v. *Heath*, 7 B. & C. 517; 1 M. & R. 335; *Blandy* v. *Allan*, 3 C. & P. 44; Danson & Lloyd, 22.

(*l*) 24 & 25 Vict. c. 96. See Appendix (2), *post*, p. 76.

(*m*) On this point see Russell on Mercantile Agency, p. 120.

the general balance of account was in his favour at the time of the pledge (*n*).

(3.) What constitutes an antecedent debt or liability.

On this subject there have been several cases arising under the 3rd section of the Factors Act, 1825, which dealt with pledges made as a security for a pre-existing "debt or demand," and the effect of the decisions given in those cases was, that there must be an actual debt owing from the agent to the pledgee at the time of the pledge, and that a mere liability of the agent which might ultimately ripen into a debt was not within the meaning of the Act.

In *Jewan* v. *Whitworth* (*o*), a factor was liable as surety to W., W. having bought goods in his own name, but on the factor's behalf. The factor deposited with W., and W. deposited with C. the bill of lading of a cargo of goods belonging to the factor's principal, on the security of which C. made advances in order to discharge W.'s indebtedness under his contracts of purchase. Held that the transaction was not a pledge in respect of an antecedent debt, because the factor was not indebted to W. at the time of the pledge, but was a pledge in respect of a *bonâ fide* advance made by C. to the factor.

In *Macnee* v. *Gorst* (*p*), a factor was liable to G. on a bill of exchange, which G. had accepted on his behalf, and also on a resale of goods made by G. at a loss, and pledged goods with G. as security in respect of these transactions. Held that *in the absence of a money advance* the transaction was not protected by the Factors Acts, and *semble* that the pledge was made in respect of an antecedent debt. Lord Hatherley said, "If I should be wrong in that view (of indebtedness), and if this should not be an antecedent debt, but only a *liability*, then I think it is a transaction which is not protected by the statute, because I read the 3rd section of 5 & 6 Vict. c. 39, as protecting nothing except an actual advance of money."

In *Kaltenbach* v. *Lewis* (*q*), M., a factor, was liable to L. on

---

(*n*) *Robertson* v. *Kensington*, 5 M. & Ry. 381.
(*o*) L. R. 2 Eq. 692.
(*p*) L. R. 4 Eq. 315.
(*q*) 10 App. Cas. 617.

the purchase of goods which L. had made on M.'s behalf. L. gave M. money to enable him to pay for the goods, and M. pledged with L. goods of his principal as security for L.'s advance. Held by the House of Lords (confirming the Court of Appeal upon this point) that the pledge was not made in respect of an antecedent debt, because at the time of the pledge M. was not indebted to L., but was only under a liability to him for the debt owing from L. to the vendors of the goods, which liability would not become a debt until after the vendors had been paid.

We have already pointed out that the language of this section differs from that of the 3rd section of the Factors Act, 1825, in providing that a valid pledge may be made to secure a "liability due" as well as a "debt due" from the pledgor to the pledgee at the time of the pledge. The expression "liability *due*" is perhaps a little ambiguous, but there can be no doubt that the Legislature intends by the phrase any liability accruing due, and not a liability already accrued due, as distinguished from a mere liability which may or may not ripen into a debt (*r*). If the words "liability due" were to receive this latter limited construction, they would be merely words of surplusage, because the term "antecedent debt" includes a liability which has accrued due, and so ripened into a debt, and this latter species of debt is only distinguishable from the former in respect of its source being a liability, and not an actual money advance. It is presumed that the liability intended is a pecuniary one, *i. e.*, a liability to pay money. This may be inferred from the 5th clause of the first section of the Act, which expressly provides that the present consideration for a pledge may be either an advance or a pecuniary liability (incurred by the pledgee) which, under the form of a past consideration with which the 4th section is concerned, become respectively, from the point of view of the pledgor, an antece-

---

(*r*) As confirmatory of this view, we may notice that in Sir J. Lubbock's Bill, upon the lines of which the present Act was drawn, an "antecedent debt" was expressly defined to include "any contingent or accruing debt, or liability previously contracted"; and Sir J. Lubbock, in introducing the Bill, referred to the intention of the framers of the Bill to amend the law in this direction.

dent debt or a pecuniary liability "due," *i.e.*, accruing due from the pledgor to the pledgee in respect of the liability previously incurred by the latter on the former's behalf. It is therefore submitted that the object of the Legislature in protecting a pre-existing liability as well as a pre-existing debt was to avoid the effect of the decisions to which we have just referred, which were based upon the distinction between a liability and a debt. Illustrations of an antecedent liability may be drawn from those cases. Thus the liability of the pledgor to the pledgee on a bill of exchange already accepted by the pledgee on the pledgor's behalf, as in *Maenee* v. *Gorst*, or the liability of the pledgor to the pledgee on purchases made by the pledgee as the pledgor's broker, as in *Jewan* v. *Whitworth*, and *Kaltenbach* v. *Lewis*, would now form a valid consideration for a pledge to the extent of the pledgor's lien on the goods, although the liability would only ripen into a debt when the pledgee had met the bill of exchange, or had paid the purchase-money to the vendors.

It is to be observed that, in order to bring a pledge within this section, it must be made to the same person to whom the pledgor is already indebted or liable. Thus the section does not apply to the case of a pledgee who *bonâ fide* advances money upon the security of the pledge, although the object of the advance may be to discharge the antecedent debt or liability of the pledgor to another person, and the pledgee is protected to the full extent of his advance under the second section of the Act (*s*).

5. The consideration necessary for the validity of a sale, pledge, or other disposition, of goods, in pursuance of this Act, may be either a payment in cash, or the delivery or transfer of other goods, or of a document of title to goods, or of a negotiable security, or any other valuable consideration; but where goods are pledged by a mercantile agent in consideration of the delivery

---

(*s*) See *Jewan* v. *Whitworth*, 2 Eq. 692.

P.   E

or transfer of other goods, or of a document of title to goods, or of a negotiable security, the pledgee shall acquire no right or interest in the goods so pledged in excess of the value of the goods, documents, or security when so delivered or transferred in exchange.

This section deals with the consideration necessary for the validity of a sale, pledge, or other disposition of goods made in pursuance of the Act, and its effect is, by widening the class of valid dispositions, to extend the application of the statute to transactions of a description which had not been protected under the earlier Factors Acts. Those enactments required, for the validity of a sale or pledge made by a factor or agent for sale, that the consideration should be a pecuniary one. By the second section of the Factors Act, 1825, which (with the fourth section of the same Act) embodied, previous to the present Act, the existing law relating to sales, a person intrusted with and in possession of a document of title was enabled to make a valid contract for the "sale *or disposition*" of goods; but it was decided, soon after the passing of the Act, that the additional word "disposition" did not enlarge the class of valid transactions, and that the disposition must be a transaction in the nature of a sale, and no protection was given to an exchange of securities (*t*).

The first section of the Factors Act, 1842, which contained the existing law relating to pledges, gave validity to any pledge made by way of security for an "original loan, advance, or payment . . . . . as also for any further or continuing advance"; and although the second section of the same Act amended the earlier law by extending protection to a *bonâ fide* exchange of securities, viz., when the agent pledges fresh securities in exchange for those originally pledged, the consideration for the pledge was treated as exceptional, and the same validity was given to the pledge " as if the consideration for the same had been a *bonâ fide* present advance of money."

(*t*) *Taylor* v. *Kymer*, 3 B. & Ad. 320, 357.

Under the earlier Factors Acts, then, a money payment, and nothing else, formed the necessary consideration for the validity of a sale or pledge made by a factor, or other agent for sale.

Now, the present section of the new Act enlarges the nature of the consideration. It may consist of :—(1) a payment in cash as before, viz., in the case of a sale, the price (*u*), or, in the case of a pledge, an advance; or (2) the delivery or transfer of other goods, or of a document of title to goods, or of a negotiable security, thus empowering the agent, by an out-and-out disposition, to barter the goods of his principal, or to pledge them in exchange for other goods or documents of title, or negotiable securities; or (3) any other valuable consideration, which must be taken to include a pecuniary liability, which is now a valid consideration for a pledge under the first (fifth clause) and fourth sections of the Act.

Now, by the common law, a factor had no authority to dispose of the goods of his principal by way of *barter*, and the principal's property in the goods was not divested by such a disposition, and he could maintain trover against the person with whom they were bartered (*x*). The effect of this section is to abrogate the common law rule on this point. It has been observed that, under the second section (first clause) of the Act, the "sale, pledge, or other disposition" must be made by the agent when acting "in the ordinary course of business of a mercantile agent." Now, to barter goods is not in the ordinary course of such an agent's business, so that a disposition by way of barter, although rendered valid by the fifth section, would not fulfil the condition imposed by the second section as necessary to its validity. This difficulty may be met by the assumption that the fifth section in effect declares that sale, for the purposes of the Act, shall include barter, although they are quite distinct transactions (*y*), when it would

---

(*u*) It is unnecessary that money should actually pass on a sale, because the buyer may set off against the price a debt due from the agent to himself. It was held, under the 4th section of the Factors Act, 1825, that the goods may be transferred for an antecedent debt: *Thackrah* v. *Fergusson*, 25 W. R. 307.

(*x*) *Guerreiro* v. *Peile*, 3 B. & Al. 616.

(*y*) See Benj. on Sale (4th ed.), p. 1.

follow that, as sale is in the ordinary course of the agent's business, barter also would be deemed to be so.

The latter portion of the section, which deals with the case of a pledge of goods made in exchange for other goods, or of a document of title, or of a negotiable security, contemplates not only a transaction which is in its inception an exchange, but also one where the agent has originally pledged goods or securities for a money advance, and afterwards substitutes other goods or securities in exchange for those originally pledged.

Here it is necessary to refer briefly to the provisions of the previous Factors Acts relating to this subject. Under the second section of the Factors Act, 1825, which provides for pledges made by persons in possession of documents of title, and which required that an advance should be made *upon the faith of* the documents deposited, it was held that a *bonâ fide* exchange of securities, the later securities being deposited as a security for the advance previously made on the security of the original securities, was not protected, on the ground that there was no advance made by the pledgee at the time of the pledge on the faith of the substituted securities. These latter were, in fact, deposited as security for an antecedent debt due from the pledgor to the pledgee. N. & Co., who were factors, purchased for the plaintiffs, their principals, certain chests of indigo, then lying in the East India Company's warehouses, for which they obtained the warrants. N. & Co. had previously borrowed money from the defendants, and had deposited with them as security other warrants for indigo. Being desirous to obtain these warrants, they deposited with the defendants in exchange the warrants for the goods belonging to the plaintiffs. The plaintiffs brought trover for these warrants, and it was held that they were entitled to recover. Lord Tenterden, who tried the action, said, in the course of his judgment: "Holding the warrants originally deposited with them as securities, the defendants give them up, and receive the warrants in question in exchange. This does not appear to me a transaction within the second section of the statute. It is no pledge or deposit of them as a security for money advanced on the faith of them; for the money for which they are a security was previously due, namely, in the former transactions, when the warrants for which they were exchanged came into the hands of the defendants" (z). The second section of the Factors Act, 1842, amended the law on this point, and provided that where an advance had been made to a factor on the security of goods, documents of title, or negotiable securities, and these are given up by the pledgee in exchange for other goods, documents of title, or negotiable securities deposited in their place, the pledgee should have a lien upon these latter to the extent of the value of the goods, documents of title, or securities delivered up in exchange, and this section of the Act re-enacts the second section of the Act of 1842.

It has been decided that the transaction will be protected although the goods or securities originally pledged have not been pledged by the agent who pledges the substituted goods or securities (a). Thus, where a person pledges goods upon the guarantee of another person, and the guarantor afterwards comes into possession of goods as a mercantile agent, and substitutes those goods in lieu of the goods originally pledged by the person for whom he was guarantor, the transaction will be protected under this section (b).

This section authorizes a mercantile agent to pledge goods in exchange for negotiable securities, which will now, having regard to the eleventh section of the Act, not only include documents, such as notes and bills, which pass by indorsement, but also other documents which are transferable by delivery only. This annuls the effect of an early decision by which East India Company's warrants were held not to be "negotiable instruments" within the meaning of the Factors Act, 1825, on the ground that they were transferable by delivery and not by indorsement (c).

There is nothing in the statute which interferes with the common law right of a mercantile agent to pledge securities which are negotiable at common law as distinguished from "documents of title," which are not negotiable except by way of estoppel. A mercantile agent can, at common law,

(z) *Taylor* v. *Trueman*, 1 Moo. & M. 453.
(a) *Sheppard* v. *Union Bank of London*, 7 H. & N. 661.
(b) *Ibid.*
(c) *Taylor* v. *Trueman*, 1 Moo. & M. 453.

pledge negotiable securities belonging to his principal, such as bills of exchange drawn in blank, for an advance made to himself, and the principal will be bound by such a pledge, provided that the pledgee acts *bonâ fide* and without notice of the pledgor's want of title (*d*).

6. For the purposes of this Act an agreement made with a mercantile agent through a clerk or other person authorized in the ordinary course of business to make contracts of sale or pledge on his behalf shall be deemed to be an agreement with the agent.

This section re-enacts a clause of the fourth section of the Act of 1842, with the additional proviso that the "clerk or other person" with whom the agreement is made shall be authorized, in the ordinary course of business, to make contracts of sale or pledge. At common law a factor or broker has no power to delegate his authority without the assent, express or implied, of his principal—"*delegatus non potest delegare*" (*e*). But if from the nature of the business, or by the usage of trade, the agent is accustomed to delegate his powers to a sub-agent, it will be inferred that the principal has impliedly authorized the delegation, and he will be bound by the contracts made by the sub-agent to the same extent as if they were made by the agent. This section is only a statutory recognition of the common law rule on this point.

7.—(1.) Where the owner of goods has given possession of the goods to another person for the purpose of consignment or sale, or has shipped the goods in the name of another person, and the consignee of the goods has not had notice that such person is not the owner of the goods,

(*d*) See Story on Agency, § 228. The 13th section of the Act expressly preserves the common law powers of the agent.

(*e*) *Solly* v. *Rathbone*, 2 M. & S. 298; *Cockrane* v. *Irlam*, 2 M. & S. 301.

the consignee shall, in respect of advances made to or for the use of such person, have the same lien on the goods as if such person were the owner of the goods, and may transfer any such lien to another person.

(2.) Nothing in this section shall limit or affect the validity of any sale, pledge, or disposition, by a mercantile agent.

This section in effect re-enacts the first section of the Factors Act, 1825, which provided that factors or agents having goods in their possession should be deemed to be the true owners so as to give validity to contracts made with consignees dealing *bonâ fide* upon the faith of such property. It only applies as between a consignor of goods and a consignee, and it confers on a consignee, who *bonâ fide* makes advances to a consignor without notice that the consignor is not the owner of the goods, the same lien upon the goods as if the ostensible had been the real owner. The owner must have *given* possession of the goods to the consignor (thereby implying the owner's consent) for the purpose of consignment or sale, *or* have shipped the goods in the consignor's name. The disjunctive "or" must, it is submitted, be equivalent to the conjunctive "and"; for, unless the goods are shipped in the consignor's name, the consignor is not the ostensible owner. The conjunctive was used in the first section of the Act of 1825. It would appear that the goods must have been shipped for the purpose of sale, and that the addition of the word "consignment" does not extend the operation of the section beyond the class of consignors for sale (*f*). The section refers expressly only to advances made, and not also, as was the case in the Factors Act, 1825, to negotiable securities given by the consignee to the consignor. This seems to be an important omission, because it is the custom for a consignee to accept bills of exchange in the consignor's favour against the cargo which is consigned to him. It would probably,

---

(*f*) See per Bramwell, L. J., in *Johnson* v. *Crédit Lyonnais Co.*, 3 C. P. D. at p. 44.

however, be held that the expression "advance" includes a payment made not only in money, but also in a bill of exchange or other negotiable security; but the Act contains no definition of the term "advance" (see sect. 4 of the Factors Act, 1842).

As to what constitutes "notice," the reader is referred to the note on the subject under the second section and first subsection of the Act. The proviso as to notice is possibly in the consignee's favour, since at common law knowledge alone, however acquired, without formal notice of the agency, would prevent the consignee from acquiring a lien over the goods (g); at the same time, it is doubtful whether knowledge, as distinguished from notice, would affect the consignee's rights.

The effect of the first clause of the section being to confer a lien on a consignee who obtains possession of goods in respect of advances made by him to the consignor, the second clause has for its object to preserve intact the validity of any sale, pledge, or disposition of the goods made by a consignor for sale, who, as such, comes within the statutory definition of a "mercantile agent," as against the claim of a consignee who has made advances to the consignor. Thus, so long as a consignor for sale, who is under advances from the consignee, remains in possession of the goods, he can make a perfectly valid sale or pledge of the goods, and the title of the purchaser or pledgee will not be affected by the consignee's claim; but if the consignee has once obtained possession of the goods his lien will prevail; for the second section of the Act only gives validity to a disposition made by a mercantile agent who is in possession.

Dispositions by Sellers and Buyers of Goods.

8. Where a person, having sold goods, continues, or is, in possession of the goods or of the documents of title to the goods, the delivery or transfer by that person, or by a mercantile agent acting for him, of the goods or documents of title under any sale, pledge, or other disposition

---

(g) See per Lord Blackburn in *Mildred* v. *Maspons*, 8 App. Cas. 885.

thereof, or under any agreement for sale, pledge, or other disposition thereof, to any person receiving the same in good faith and without notice of the previous sale, shall have the same effect as if the person making the delivery or transfer were expressly authorized by the owner of the goods to make the same.

The effect of this section is to extend the doctrine of ostensible ownership to the particular case of a seller who is allowed by a buyer to remain in possession of the goods sold, or of the documents of title thereto. When a seller under these circumstances resells, or pledges, or otherwise disposes of the goods, the title of the person who *bonâ fide*, and without notice of the previous sale, receives the goods, or the documents of title relating to them under the resale, pledge, or other disposition, will prevail over the title of the original buyer.

The case of a seller allowed by a buyer to remain in possession of the goods sold was not provided for, either by the common law or by the three earliest Factors Acts. At common law the doctrine of estoppel only applied where the owner of goods had *acted* so as to clothe the seller with apparent authority to sell or pledge them, and not to a case like the one under consideration, where the owner had only remained *passive;* and the Factors Acts only applied to the case of an "agent intrusted with the goods," whereas the seller was not the buyer's agent. The point, however, did not come before the Courts for adjudication until the year 1877.

In *Johnson* v. *The Crédit Lyonnais Co.* (*h*), one H. was a tobacco broker and importer. H. sold tobacco to the plaintiff; the tobacco remaining in bond in H.'s name, and H. retaining in his possession the dock warrants, and being entered in the dock company's books as owner. The plaintiff, not wishing to clear the tobacco out of bond at once, took no steps to have it transferred into his name in the dock company's books. After the sale to the plaintiff, H. fraudulently pledged the goods, and

(*h*) 2 C. P. D. 224; on appeal, 3 C. P. D. 32.

handed over the warrants to the defendants, who gave notice to the dock company of the change of ownership. It was held that the plaintiff was entitled to recover the tobacco from the defendants, on the grounds (1) that H. was not an agent "intrusted" with the goods or the documents of title relating to them, so that the pledge made by him was not protected by the Factors Acts, 1825 and 1842; and (2) that the plaintiff was not estopped from asserting his title to the tobacco because he had no knowledge of the dealing with his property, which was essential to establish an estoppel. The Court further held that the plaintiff was not estopped by his negligence, because he was under no duty to the defendants. This decision caused great alarm among merchants, and the law was immediately amended by the Factors Act, 1877. The Act proceeded on the view that the buyer, in leaving the documents in the possession of the seller, and in omitting to have the goods transferred to his own name, was guilty of negligence, and that, therefore, as between two innocent parties, he ought to suffer.

This section, while substantially re-enacting the third section of the Act of 1877, so far as it altered the law as laid down in *Johnson* v. *The Crédit Lyonnais Co.*, amends the earlier statute in some important particulars: (1.) The Act of 1877 only provided for the case of a seller who continued to be or was in possession of a document of title to goods; this section extends its operation to the case where the goods are in the seller's possession. There is this important distinction between the two cases: when the goods are represented by a document of title, the buyer who finds it necessary or convenient in the course of business to leave the document in the seller's possession, may secure himself against the seller's fraudulently making a subsequent disposition of the goods by having the document specially indorsed to himself, and when the goods are in the possession of a wharfinger or warehouseman, by having the goods entered in his (the buyer's) name; while, on the other hand, when the actual goods are left in the seller's possession, it will be necessary for the buyer so to earmark the particular goods sold—*e. g.*, by having them marked with his own name—as to prevent the seller from continuing to be the ostensible owner. In some cases this may be a matter of difficulty, so that the buyer will only be able to protect himself against the possibility of fraudulent dealing with the goods by obtaining an immediate delivery of the goods to himself.

(2.) The Act of 1877 applied, although possibly not intended to do so, not only when the second buyer or the pledgee had the document of title transferred to him, but also when the disposition was made without any transfer of the document; so that the person dealing with the seller might even be ignorant that the document was in the seller's possession. This section gives validity to a disposition only in the case where the goods or the document of title have been actually delivered or transferred to the second buyer or the pledgee. This is an important amendment of the law. There seems to be no reason why the title of the second buyer or the pledgee of the goods, who has not obtained possession of the goods or of the document of title thereto, should be preferred to that of the first buyer; on the contrary, the maxim "*Qui prior est tempore, potior est jure,*" applies, since neither party has acquired a legal title, and the title of the first buyer ought to be preferred.

It is important to observe that this section, following the third section of the Factors Act, 1877, applies not only when the seller has been left by the buyer in possession of the goods or of a document of title, but also when the seller has got possession of them *after* the sale, the words of the section being when the seller "continues or is in possession."

With regard to notice, the second buyer or the pledgee may be fixed with notice of the previous sale either—(1) *directly*, from communication or from the fact of the goods being marked or otherwise appropriated to the first buyer, or from the evidence of the document of title itself, when the goods are transferred by means of a document; for the subsequent disposition of the goods will be rendered valid only when the document shows on its face that the goods are deliverable to the seller; or (2) *indirectly*, from knowledge of circumstances which would lead a reasonable man of business to the conclusion that a sale of the goods had already taken place (*i*).

. (*i*) *Evans* v. *Trueman*, 1 Moo. & Rob. 10, *ante*, p. 40.

9. Where a person, having bought or agreed to buy goods, obtains with the consent of the seller possession of the goods or the documents of title to the goods, the delivery or transfer, by that person or by a mercantile agent acting for him, of the goods or documents of title, under any sale, pledge, or other disposition thereof, or under any agreement for sale, pledge, or other disposition thereof, to any person receiving the same in good faith and without notice of any lien or other right of the original seller in respect of the goods, shall have the same effect as if the person making the delivery or transfer were a mercantile agent in possession of the goods or documents of title with the consent of the owner.

This section provides for the converse case to that provided for by the preceding section, viz., a buyer allowed by the seller to obtain possession of the goods sold, or of the documents of title relating to them; and its effect is to give, under these circumstances, the same validity to a sale, pledge, or other disposition of the goods by the buyer, when accompanied by a delivery or transfer of the goods or of the document of title, as the second section of the Act gives to a similar disposition when made by a mercantile agent in possession of the goods with the owner's consent. The person dealing with a buyer so in possession must act *bonâ fide* throughout, and have no notice of the existing lien or other right of the original seller in respect of the goods.

In this class of cases the element of fraud is absent; the person disposing of the goods is not the ostensible only, but the actual owner of them; but the original seller may have a lien for the unpaid price, and the section provides, in effect, that the title of a *bonâ fide* transferee from the buyer shall prevail over this claim, and that the effect of the transfer shall be to defeat the original vendor's rights.

It is not necessary, in order that the section should be applicable, that there should be a memorandum of the original contract of sale of the goods, so as to satisfy the Statute of Frauds; it is sufficient that there should be a *de facto* contract of sale, under which the buyer has obtained from the seller possession of a document of title (*l*).

This section differs from the fourth section of the Factors Act, 1877, which it otherwise substantially re-enacts, in two particulars: (1) It applies, as the last preceding section, to the case of a buyer who obtains possession of the actual goods sold, as well as of a document of title relating to them, whereas the fourth section of the Factors Act, 1877, applied only to the case of a buyer in possession of a document of title. The addition of these words, however, seems to be nugatory, and not to extend the real operation of the section; because when the buyer has once obtained possession of the goods, the original seller's rights over them, which exist only until the buyer has obtained actual possession, are lost, so that a transferee from the buyer has no longer any need for the protection which the section affords. (2) The section applies only when there has been a delivery or transfer of the goods, or of a document of title, while the fourth section, if literally read, applied to a sale, pledge, or other disposition of the goods, even when unaccompanied by a transfer of the documents of title relating to them.

The Factors Acts, previous to the Act of 1877, had not provided for the case of a buyer allowed to have possession of documents of title, and by several decisions given under those Acts it was settled that the words "an agent intrusted with goods or documents of title" did not include a buyer, because he held in his own right and not as agent (*m*). The singular anomaly thus existed, as was pointed out by Mr. Benjamin in the Treatise on Sale (*n*), that if a merchant, buying goods and paying the price, received a transfer of the dock warrant, he would be safe if his vendor was *not owner*, but only agent of the assignor of the warrant, and would not be safe if the vendor *was owner*, because the price might remain unpaid by

---

(*l*) *Hugill* v. *Masker*, 22 Q. B. D. 364.

(*m*) *Jenkyns* v. *Usborne*, 7 M. & G. 678; *Van Casteel* v. *Booker*, 2 Ex. 671; *Fuentes* v. *Montis*, L. R. 3 C. P. 268.

(*n*) Benj. on Sale (4th ed. by the Author and Mr. H. F. Boyd), p. 831.

the assignor of the warrant, who would then have a lien upon the goods for the price. This result followed from the difference between the common law and the statutory conception of a "document of title." By the common law, "dock warrants, warehouse-keepers' certificates, warrants, or orders for the delivery of goods," were regarded as mere "tokens of authority to receive possession," and a transfer of one of these documents did not *per se* divest the seller's lien, but was incomplete until the buyer had obtained the assent of the warehouseman or wharfinger to attorn to him. By statute, on the other hand, these documents were treated as "instruments used in the ordinary course of business as proof of the possession or control of goods," and as "authorizing the *possessor* of such document to transfer *goods thereby represented*." (See the fourth section of the Factors Act, 1842.) In a word, the Legislature dealt with these documents as being, like a bill of lading, the *symbols* of the goods which they represent.

Under the eighth, ninth and tenth sections of this Act these documents will receive the statutory interpretation when transferred by a seller or buyer who is allowed to have possession of them, to a *bonâ fide* transferee for value, but they will still receive the common law interpretation in transactions which lie outside the scope of the Factors Act. Thus, *e. g.*, the transfer of one of these documents directly from a seller to a buyer will not, like the transfer of a bill of lading, divest the seller's lien; in order to effect that, the person in whose custody the goods are must attorn to the buyer, or the latter must take actual possession of the goods (*post*, p. 68).

10. Where a document of title to goods has been lawfully transferred to a person as a buyer or owner of the goods, and that person transfers the document to a person who takes the document in good faith and for valuable consideration, the last-mentioned transfer shall have the same effect for defeating any vendor's lien or right of stoppage in transitu as the transfer of a bill of lading has for defeating the right of stoppage in transitu.

We have already observed that this section seems to include the particular case already provided for by the preceding section, which deals specifically with the position of a buyer obtaining possession of goods, or of a document of title thereto; while this section contemplates the effect upon the vendor's rights of the transfer of a document of title by a person to whom such document has been lawfully transferred "as buyer or owner." It may be useful to compare the language of the two sections; for although they both apparently contemplate dispositions of goods made under similar circumstances, they appear, upon comparison, to differ in their respective requirements and effect. The ninth section applies to a buyer who has obtained possession of a document of title (*o*) with the seller's consent; the tenth section applies to a person to whom a document of title has been transferred "as a buyer or owner of the goods." As the section operates solely in defeating an unpaid seller's lien or right of stoppage *in transitu*, the original transfer must be from a seller to a buyer, or from a *quasi*-seller—*e.g.*, a consignor—to a consignee. The consignor who has bought goods on his own credit, but on his principal's account, is in the same position as a seller *quoad* his principal, and can exercise a seller's rights; and it is probable that by a transfer to one "as owner of the goods" the section contemplates this case. The section, therefore, applies to a buyer or consignee who has obtained possession of a document of title from a seller or consignor of the goods (the transfer being effected either by indorsement or mere delivery), so that it includes the particular case provided for by the ninth section, of a buyer obtaining possession of a document of title with the seller's consent.

Let us next consider what each section respectively requires for the validity of a sale, pledge, or disposition made by the person so in possession of a document of title. Under the ninth section the transferee must receive the document "in

---

(*o*) For the purpose of comparison, the case of the buyer's possession of the actual goods, included in the ninth section is omitted.

good faith, and without notice of any lien or other right (*i.e.*, stoppage *in transitu*) of the original seller in respect of the goods;" while under the tenth section the transferee must take the document "in good faith and for valuable consideration." The ninth section, therefore, contains a proviso as to notice which is not contained in the tenth. Now, it has long been settled that the transfer of a bill of lading will defeat the vendor's lien, although the transferee may have notice that the goods have not been paid for (q), and that a transfer "in good faith" only requires that the transferee is without notice of such circumstances as render the bill of lading not fairly and honestly assignable (r). It follows, therefore, that whereas under the tenth section, which gives to the transfer of all documents of title the same effect for defeating the vendor's rights as the transfer of a bill of lading formerly had, notice to the transferee that the goods have not been paid for, and, consequently, knowledge on his part of the existence of the unpaid vendor's lien or other right will not invalidate the transaction. On the other hand, under the ninth section, notice of the original vendor's lien or other right will have that effect. Again, since, under the ninth section, the transfer by the buyer is to have the same effect as though he were a mercantile agent under the second section of the Act, the original seller's rights will be totally defeated thereby, whether the transaction be a sale or a pledge; whereas under the tenth section, as will be shown later, the transfer of a document of title by way of pledge will defeat the unpaid seller's rights in part only, and to the extent necessary in order to give effect to the pledgee's interest. In the absence of any judicial decision upon the effect of the fourth and fifth sections of the Factors Act, 1877, it is impossible to pronounce beforehand upon the interpretation which the Courts will place upon the provisions of the ninth and tenth sections of this Act, if and when a case arises for adjudication; and it must suffice here to have called attention to the variance in language, and difference in effect, of these two sections when seemingly dealing with a precisely similar set of circumstances.

(q) *Cuming* v. *Brown*, 9 East, 506.
(r) *Salomons* v. *Nissen*, 2 T. R. 681.

The direct object of the section now under consideration is to give to a transfer of any "document of title," as defined by the first section (fourth sub-section) of the Act, when made by a buyer to a *bonâ fide* transferee for value from him, the same effect for defeating the original seller's lien or right of stoppage *in transitu*, as the transfer of a bill of lading has, at common law, for defeating the right of stoppage *in transitu*.

Now, at common law, a bill of lading is not negotiable like a bank note or bill of exchange. It is not strictly a document of title at all in the sense that the holder derives his title from the instrument itself, and not from the title of the person from whom he received it. The assignor of a bill of lading must have a title to the goods, or authority to act for one who has. An assignor who is a mere holder of the document, or who has found or stolen it, can transfer no interest to the assignee in the goods represented thereby. It is submitted that the expression "lawfully transferred" in this section, although, perhaps, not altogether free from ambiguity, means that the transferor of any of the so-called "documents of title" must have, as in the case of the transferor of a bill of lading, a title to the goods represented by the document. When this condition was fulfilled, the transfer of a bill of lading had, at common law, the same effect as the actual delivery of the goods, and completely divested the seller's lien. But as between an original seller and a buyer of the goods, the transfer of a bill of lading did not prevent the seller from exercising his right of stoppage *in transitu* upon the insolvency of the buyer, provided that the goods had not reached the actual possession of the buyer, or that he had not in the meanwhile transferred the bill of lading to a *bonâ fide* transferee for value. But it was decided in the great leading case of *Lickbarrow* v. *Mason* (s) that the seller's right of stoppage *in transitu* was defeated by the buyer's negotiation of the bill of lading with a *bonâ fide* indorsee, and the effect of this section is to extend the principle of *Lickbarrow* v. *Mason* (s), which was confined by that case to the transfer of a bill of lading, to the transfer of any document of title as defined by the first section of the Act.

(s) 1 Smith, L. C. (1887). 737.

At common law, in order to defeat the seller's right, the indorsement must be *bonâ fide* and for value, and this section confirms the common law by requiring that the transferee shall take the document "in good faith and for valuable consideration." By good faith is meant, not without notice that the goods are unpaid for, because a man may be perfectly honest in dealing for goods that he knows not to have been paid for (*s*), but without knowledge of such circumstances as would make the document of title not fairly and honestly assignable, *e.g.*, knowledge of the insolvency of the vendee or assignee (*t*).

"For valuable consideration" will, apparently, include a transfer made in consideration of a pre-existing debt (*u*).

When the goods were resold by the buyer, and the bill of lading was transferred on the resale to the second buyer, the effect of the transfer was to destroy the original seller's right of stoppage *in transitu*; but when the bill of lading was transferred by way of pledge, the seller's right was defeated in part only, and he was still entitled to any surplus proceeds of the sale of the goods after the pledgee's claim had been satisfied, and he had the further equitable right of insisting upon the pledgee's marshalling the assets (*x*).

Now, with reference to the documents enumerated in the first section as "documents of title," we have already stated that, independently of the Factors Acts, the transfer of a delivery order or a dock warrant had no effect beyond that of a mere offer or token of authority to receive possession, and did not, like a bill of lading, actually transfer the possession. With regard to a delivery order, it was well settled that delivery was not complete until the bailee attorned to the buyer, and became the latter's agent as custodian of the goods (*y*). It was also settled that the transfer of a delivery order by a buyer to a sub-vendee differed in effect from that

---

(*s*) *Cuming* v. *Brown*, 9 East, 506.

(*t*) *Salomons* v. *Nissen*, 2 T. R. 681; *Vertue* v. *Jewell*, 4 Camp. 31.

(*u*) *Leask* v. *Scott*, 2 Q. B. D. 376, where the Court of Appeal disapproved of a decision to the contrary by the Privy Council in *Rodger* v. *Comptoir d'Escompte*, L. R. 2 P. C. 393; 38 L. J. P. C. 30.

(*x*) *In re Westzinthus*, 5 B. & Ad. 817; *Spalding* v. *Ruding*, 6 Bea. 376; *Kemp* v. *Falk*, 7 App. Cas. 573.

(*y*) *Bentall* v. *Burn*, 3 B. & C. 423.

of a bill of lading, and did not affect the original seller's lien, when neither the original buyer nor the sub-vendee had procured the acceptance of the order nor taken actual possession of the goods before the order was countermanded (z).

Contrasting the effect of a transfer of dock warrants, wharfingers' receipts, delivery orders, and similar documents with that of a bill of lading, Lord Blackburn remarks that "these documents are generally written contracts, by which the holder of the indorsed document is rendered the person to whom the holder of the goods is to deliver them, and in so far they greatly resemble bills of lading; but they differ from them in this respect, that when goods are at sea, the purchaser who takes the bill of lading has done all that is possible in order to take possession of the goods, as there is a physical obstacle to his seeking out the master of the ship, and requiring him to attorn to his right; but when the goods are on land, there is no reason why the person who receives a delivery order or dock warrant should not at once lodge it with the bailee, and so take actual or constructive possession of the goods. There is, therefore, a very sufficient reason why the custom of merchants should make the transfer of the bill of lading equivalent to an actual delivery of possession, and yet not give such an effect to the transfer of documents of title to goods on shore. Besides this substantial difference between them, there is the more technical one that bills of lading are ancient mercantile documents, which may be subject to the law merchant; whilst the other class of documents are of modern invention, and no custom of merchants relating to them has ever been established" (a).

With regard to dock warrants and certificates, special juries of London merchants have repeatedly testified that they treated a transfer of these documents as an actual transfer of the possession of the goods they represent; on the other hand, we believe that it has never been the custom of merchants to treat delivery orders in the same way. In the ordinary course of business, a delivery order is presented to the warehouseman

---

(z) *M'Ewan* v. *Smith*, 2 H. of L. C. 309; *Griffiths* v. *Perry*, 1 E. & E. 680; *Farina* v. *Horne*, 16 M. & W. 119.

(a) Blackburn on Sale (2nd ed.), p. 415.

or wharfinger who has the custody of the goods, and exchanged for a warrant; but the goods having then already reached their destination, the negotiation of the delivery order could have no effect on the seller's right of stoppage *in transitu*.

But this section, by extending the effect given at common law to the transfer of a bill of lading to that of any "document of title," including both a delivery order and a warrant, provides (1) that on a *resale* of goods by a buyer or consignee, accompanied by a transfer of a document of title to the sub-purchaser, the original vendor's lien or right of stoppage *in transitu* will be at once divested without attornment by the warehouseman, wharfinger, or other custodian of the goods; but (2) that when the buyer or consignee has transferred a document of title by way of *pledge*, the vendor's lien will, as it is submitted, be divested in fact, and not necessarily *in toto*, but will exist so far as it is enforceable without prejudice to the pledgee's interest, this being the effect of the transfer of a bill of lading at common law upon the seller's right of stoppage *in transitu*.

As between a seller and buyer, the distinction which was drawn at common law between the effect of a transfer of a bill of lading, and of a delivery order, dock warrant, or other like document, remains unaffected by this section, and a transfer of one of the last-mentioned documents will not divest the vendor's lien unless and until the warehouseman, wharfinger, or other custodian of the goods attorns to the buyer, or the latter takes actual possession of the goods.

We believe that there are no reported decisions in which the corresponding section of the Factors Act, 1877, has been discussed, and which might serve as guides to the judicial construction likely to be placed upon this section.

It was, indeed, argued, in *Kemp* v. *Falk* (*b*), that cash receipts given by a vendee to a sub-purchaser, upon the presentation of which the latter was entitled to receive goods from the master of the ship, were documents of title equivalent to delivery orders, and that accordingly there was a transfer or delivery of the goods, within the meaning of the fifth section of the Factors Act, 1877, sufficient to defeat the

(*b*) 7 App. Cas. 573.

vendor's right of stoppage *in transitu.* This contention was at once overruled by Lord Blackburn, who states that he only notices it on account of the great importance attaching to all that relates to the Factors Acts.

Supplemental.

11. For the purposes of this Act, the transfer of a document may be by indorsement, or, where the document is by custom or by its express terms transferable by delivery, or makes the goods deliverable to the bearer, then by delivery.

This section reproduces a clause of the fifth section of the Factors Act, 1877.

12.—(1.) Nothing in this Act shall authorize an agent to exceed or depart from his authority as between himself and his principal, or exempt him from any liability, civil or criminal, for so doing.

The object of the Legislature in the Factors Acts is not to authorize an agent to sell or pledge another man's property, or to deviate from the authority he has received from his principal; the agent, therefore, remains civilly and criminally responsible for any breach of duty committed in the course of his employment.

The criminal liability of the agent was provided for by the seventh and following sections of the Factors Act, 1825, and by the sixth section of the Factors Act, 1842.

These provisions are now superseded by the Larceny Act, 1861 (24 & 25 Vict. c. 96), the material sections of which will be found in Appendix 2, *post,* p. 75.

(2.) Nothing in this Act shall prevent the owner of goods from recovering the goods from an agent or his trustee in bankruptcy at any time before the sale or pledge thereof, or shall prevent the owner of goods pledged by an agent from having the right to redeem the goods at any time before the sale thereof, on satisfying the claim for which the goods were pledged, and paying to the agent, if by him required, any money in respect of which the agent would by law be entitled to retain the goods or the documents of title thereto, or any of them, by way of lien as against the owner, or from recovering from any person with whom the goods have been pledged any balance of money remaining in his hands as the produce of the sale of the goods after deducting the amount of his lien.

(3.) Nothing in this Act shall prevent the owner of goods sold by an agent from recovering from the buyer the price agreed to be paid for the same, or any part of that price, subject to any right of set off on the part of the buyer against the agent.

These clauses reproduce the seventh section of the Factors Act, 1842 (with which compare the sixth section of the Factors Act, 1825).

They preserve the right of the real owner of goods under the following circumstances:—

1. *Before a sale or pledge by the agent.*—The owner may recover the goods from the agent or his trustee in bankruptcy (*c*).

2. *After a pledge by the agent, and before a sale by the pledgee.*—The owner may redeem the goods subject to his satisfying (i) the claim of the pledgee, and (ii) the claim, if

(*c*) A factor being regarded as a trustee of property in his hands as factor, such property does not pass to his trustee in bankruptcy: *Copeman* v. *Gallant*, 1 P. Wms. 314.

any, of the agent (*e.g.*, in respect of advances made or negotiable instruments given to his principal), and in respect of which the agent would be entitled to a lien on the goods or the documents of title thereto.

3. *After a sale by the pledgee.*—The owner may recover from the pledgee the balance of the proceeds of sale after deducting the amount of the pledgee's lien (*d*).

4. *After a sale by the agent.*—The owner may recover from the buyer the price agreed to be paid, or any part thereof, subject to any right of set-off which the buyer may have against the agent. With regard to the right of set-off, if the agent sells or consigns goods for an undisclosed principal, the buyer or consignee may set off any demand he may have against the agent against the demand made for the goods by the principal, and such set-off, to be available, need not exist at the time of the sale, but may arise at any time before the disclosure of the actual principal (*e*). But it is equally well settled that this rule does not apply if the person dealing with the agent knows him to have a principal, although the name of the principal may not be disclosed; and it is immaterial whether the principal carries on business in this country or abroad (*f*).

Although there is no privity of contract between the foreign principal and persons dealing with the principal's commission-agent in this country (*g*), the foreign principal has the same right as a principal residing in this country to recover goods, or their proceeds, under this section, and may maintain an action for that purpose, his right depending, not on agency, nor on privity of contract, but upon property (*h*).

13. The provisions of this Act shall be construed in amplification and not in derogation

---

(*d*) As to the owner's right to marshal securities, see *Ex parte Alston*, 4 Ch. App. 168.

(*e*) *George* v. *Clagett*, 7 T. R. 359; 2 Sm. L. C. (1887), p. 130, citing *Rabone* v. *Williams*.

(*f*) *Semenza* v. *Brinsley*, 18 C. B. (N. S.) 467; *Mildred* v. *Maspons*, 9 Q. B. D. 874; confirmed by the H. L. 8 App. Cas. 874.

(*g*) Per Lord Blackburn in *Armstrong* v. *Stokes*, L. R. 7 Q. B. at p. 605.

(*h*) *Mildred* v. *Maspons*, 8 App. Cas. 874.

of the powers exerciseable by an agent independently of this Act.

14. The enactments mentioned in the schedule to this Act are hereby repealed as from the commencement of this Act, but this repeal shall not affect any right acquired or liability incurred before the commencement of this Act under any enactment hereby repealed.

This section repeals the Factors Acts, 1823 to 1877, but the repeal is not to have a retrospective operation.

15. This Act shall commence and come into operation on the first day of January, 1890.

16. This Act shall not extend to Scotland.

This section was not included in the original bill, but was added as an amendment in Committee of the House of Commons.

There was some doubt whether the previous Factors Acts applied to Scotland (*i*). The point was raised on the pleadings in the Scotch cases of *M'Ewan* v. *Smith* (*j*), and *Pochin* v. *Robinow* (*k*), but the Courts avoided the question. By the law of Scotland, as we have already pointed out, the possession of moveables constitutes title; and it is doubtful if the Factors Acts, in the view taken of them by English judges, as not interfering with the doctrine of apparent ownership, but only investing a special class of agents with a statutory authority, would, even if applicable, have modified the existing law of Scotland (*l*).

17. This Act may be cited as the Factors Act, 1889.

(*i*) Notice the reference in the 7th section of the Factors Act, 1825, to "any part of the United Kingdom."

(*j*) 2 H. & C. 309.

(*k*) 7 Macph. 622 (1869).

(*l*) The question is fully discussed in Bell's Commentaries on the Law of Scotland, Vol. I. (7th ed.) p. 517.

APPENDIX No. 1.

1. LAW OF FRANCE—CODE NAPOLÉON.

Article 2279.

In the case of moveables, possession is equivalent to a title (possession vaut titre).

Nevertheless, the party who has lost anything, or from whom it has been stolen, may reclaim it, within three years from the day of the loss or robbery, against the party in whose hands he finds it; saving to the latter his remedy against the person from whom he obtained it.

Article 2280.

If the actual possessor of the thing stolen, or lost, has purchased it in a fair or market, or at a public sale, or from a shopkeeper(a) dealing in similar articles, the original owner can only have it restored to him on repaying the possessor the price which it cost him.

2. LAW OF GERMANY—ALLGEMEINES DEUTSCHES HANDELSGESETZBUCH (GERMAN GENERAL COMMERCIAL CODE).

Article 306.

Sale.—If goods or other moveables are disposed of and transferred by a trader (Kaufmann)(b), in the course of his

---

(a) Marchand—not a merchant in the English sense of the term, for which the French is commerçant.

(b) Art. 4 of the Code: "'Trader' (Kaufmann), in this code, means a person who carries on business in manner customary in his particular trade."

business, a *bonâ fide* transferee acquires the ownership thereof, even where the transferor was not owner. Ownership based on a prior title is extinguished. Every prior right of pledge or other right *in rem* is extinguished, if it was unknown to the transferee at the time of transfer.

Pledge.—If goods or other moveables are pledged and transferred by a trader in the course of his business, all rights of ownership, rights of pledge, or other rights *in rem* founded on prior title, cannot be enforced to the disadvantage of the *bonâ fide* (redlich) pledgee or his successor in title.

The right of lien by law given to commission agents, forwarding agents, and carriers, is of equal force to a right of pledge acquired by contract.

This article does not apply if the goods were stolen or lost.

Article 307.

The provisions of the last preceding article apply to securities (Papiere) negotiable to bearer, even where the transfer or pledge is not made by a trader in the course of his business, and where the securities (Papiere) were stolen or lost.

Article 308.

Local enactments (Landesgesetze) (*c*), which contain provisions still more favourable to the possessor, are not affected by the two last preceding articles.

Article 309.

The formalities prescribed by the Municipal Code for validly effecting a mortgage are not necessary where the mutual dealings of traders call for a pledge of moveables, securities to bearer, or securities negotiable by indorsement.

In such case, in addition to the simple agreement to pledge, it is sufficient:—

(1) In the case of moveables and securities to bearer, to transfer possession to the creditor in manner prescribed by the Municipal Code for a mortgage (thereof);

(2) In the case of securities negotiable by indorsement, to hand over the security indorsed.

(*c*) This word means the laws of any of the various States federated under Imperial rule.

APPENDIX No. 2.

LARCENY ACT, 1861.

24 & 25 Vict. c. 96.

The following sections of the Act deal with misappropriation by factors or agents:—

Sect. 78. Whosoever, *being a factor or agent intrusted*, either solely or jointly with any other person, for the purpose of sale or otherwise, with the possession of any goods, or of any document of title (*a*) to goods, shall, contrary to or without the authority of his principal in that behalf, for his own use or benefit, or the use or benefit of any person other than the person by whom he was so intrusted, and in violation of good faith, make any consignment, deposit, transfer, or delivery of any goods or document of title so intrusted to him as in this section before mentioned, as and by way of a pledge, lien, or security for any money or valuable security borrowed or received by such factor or agent at or before the time of making such consignment, deposit, transfer, or delivery, or intended to be thereafter borrowed or received, or shall, contrary to or without such authority, for his own use or benefit, or the use or benefit of any person other than the person by whom he was so intrusted, and in violation of good faith, accept any advance of any money or valuable security on the faith of any contract or agreement to consign, deposit, transfer, or deliver any such goods or document of title, shall be guilty of a misdemeanor, and being convicted thereto shall be liable, at the discretion of the Court, to any

---

(*a*) Document of title is, by section 1 of the Act, defined to include "any bill of lading, *India warrant*, dock warrant, warehouse-keeper's certificate, warrant or order for delivery *or transfer* of any goods *or valuable thing, bought and sold note*, or any other document used in the ordinary course of business as proof of the possession or control of goods, or authorizing or purporting to authorize, either by indorsement or by delivery, the possessor of such document to transfer or receive any goods thereby represented *or therein mentioned or referred to*." This definition closely corresponds with that given in the first section of the Factors Act, with which it should be compared. The italicised portions are omitted in the Factors Act.

of the punishments which the Court may award as hereinbefore last mentioned; and every clerk or other person who shall knowingly and wilfully act and assist in making any such consignment, deposit, transfer, or delivery, or in accepting or procuring such advance as aforesaid, shall be guilty of a misdemeanor, and being convicted thereof shall be liable, at the discretion of the Court, to any of the same punishments: Provided, that no such factor or agent shall be liable to any prosecution for consigning, depositing, transferring, or delivering any such goods or documents of title, in case the same shall not be made a security for or subject to the payment of any greater sum of money than the amount which at the time of such consignment, deposit, transfer, or delivery was justly due and owing to such agent from his principal, together with the amount of any bill of exchange drawn by or on account of such principal, and accepted by such factor or agent (b).

Sect. 79. Any factor or agent intrusted as aforesaid, and possessed of any such document of title, whether derived immediately from the owner of such goods or obtained by reason of such factor or agent having been intrusted with the possession of the goods or of any other document of title thereto, shall be deemed to have been intrusted with the possession of the goods represented by such document of title; and every contract pledging or giving a lien upon such document of title as aforesaid shall be deemed to be a pledge of and lien upon the goods to which the same relates; and such factor or agent shall be deemed to be possessed of such goods or document, whether the same shall be in his actual custody, or shall be held by any other person subject to his control, or for him, or on his behalf; and where any loan or advance shall be *bonâ fide* made to any factor or agent intrusted with and in possession of any such goods or documents of title, on the faith of any contract or agreement in writing to consign, deposit, transfer or deliver such goods or document of title, and such goods or document of title shall actually be received by the person making such loan or advance, without notice that such factor or agent was not authorized to make such pledge or security, every such loan or advance shall be deemed to be a loan or advance on the security of such goods or document of title within the meaning of the last preceding section, though such goods or document of title shall not actually be received by the person making such loan or advance till the period subsequent thereto; and any contract or agreement, whether made direct with such factor or agent,

---

(b) As to the factor's right to add to his lien the amount covered by unmatured acceptances, see *ante*, p. 46.

or with any clerk or other person on his behalf, shall be deemed a contract or agreement with such factor or agent; and any payment made, whether by money or bill of exchange or other negotiable security, shall be deemed to be an advance within the meaning of the last preceding section; and a factor or agent in possession as aforesaid of such goods or document shall be taken for the purposes of the last preceding section to have been intrusted therewith by the owner thereof, unless the contrary be shown in evidence (*c*).

Sect. 85. Nothing in any of the last ten preceding sections of this Act contained shall enable or entitle any person to refuse [to make a full and complete discovery by answer to any bill in equity, or] to answer any question or interrogatory in any civil proceeding in any Court, or upon the hearing of any matter in bankruptcy or insolvency; and no person shall be liable to be convicted of any of the misdemeanors in any of the said sections mentioned by any evidence whatever in respect of any act done by him, if he shall at any time previously to his being charged with such offence have first disclosed such act on oath, in consequence of any compulsory process of any Court of law or equity, in any action, suit, or proceeding which shall have been *bonâ fide* instituted by any party aggrieved, or if he shall have first disclosed the same in any compulsory examination or deposition before any Court upon the hearing of any matter in bankruptcy or insolvency (*d*).

Sect. 86. Nothing in any of the last eleven preceding sections of this Act contained, nor any proceeding, conviction or judgment to be had or taken thereon against any person under any of the said sections, shall prevent, lessen or impeach any remedy at law or in equity which any party aggrieved by any offence against any of the said sections might have had if this Act had not been passed; but no conviction of any such offender shall be received in evidence in any action at law or [suit] in equity against him; and nothing in the said sections contained shall affect or prejudice any agreement entered into or security given by any trustee, having for its object the restoration or payment of any trust property misappropriated.

Sect. 87. No misdemeanor against any of the last twelve preceding sections of this Act shall be prosecuted or tried at any Court of general or quarter sessions of the peace.

(*c*) This section is copied almost verbatim from the fourth section of the Factors Act, 1842.
(*d*) See *R.* v. *Sheen*, Bell's C. C. 97.

APPENDIX No. 3.

THE FACTORS ACTS, 1823—1877.
(*Now Repealed by the Factors Act,* 1889.)

4 GEO. 4, c. 83.

An Act for the better Protection of the Property of Merchants and others, who may hereafter enter into Contracts or Agreements in relation to Goods, Wares, or Merchandizes intrusted to Factors or Agents. [18th July, 1823.]

"WHEREAS it has been found that the law, as it now stands, relating to goods shipped in the names of persons who are not the actual proprietors thereof, and to the deposit or pledge of goods, affords great facility to fraud, produces frequent litigation, and proves, in its effects, highly injurious to the interests of commerce in general;" be it therefore enacted by the King's most excellent Majesty, by and with the advice and consent of the Lords spiritual and temporal, and Commons in this present Parliament assembled, and by the authority of the same, that from and after the passing of this Act, any person or persons intrusted, for the purpose of sale, with any goods, wares, or merchandize, and by whom such goods, wares, or merchandize shall be shipped, in his, her, or their own name or names, or in whose name or names any goods, wares, or merchandize, shall be shipped by any other person or persons, shall be deemed and taken to be the true owner or owners thereof, so far as to entitle the consignee or consignees of such goods, wares, or merchandize to a lien thereon, in respect of any money or negotiable security or securities advanced or given by such consignee or consignees, to or for the use of the person or persons in whose name or names such goods, wares, or merchandize shall be shipped, or in respect of any money or negotiable security or securities received by him, her, or them to the use of such consignee or consignees, in the like manner to all intents and purposes as if such person or persons was or were the true owner or owners of such goods, wares, and merchandize; provided such consignee or consignees shall not have notice, by the bill of lading for the delivery of such goods, wares, or merchandize, or otherwise, at or before the time of any advance of such money or negotiable security, or of such receipt of money or negotiable security, in respect of which such lien is claimed, that such person or persons so shipping in his, her, or their own name or names, or in whose name or names any goods, wares, or merchandize shall be shipped by any person or persons, is or are not the actual and *bonâ fide* owner or owners, proprietor or proprietors of such goods, wares, and merchandize so shipped as aforesaid, any law, usage, or custom to the contrary thereof in any wise notwithstanding: provided also, that the person or persons in whose name or names any such goods, wares, or merchandize are so shipped as aforesaid, shall be taken for the purposes of this Act to have been intrusted therewith, unless the contrary thereof shall appear or be shown in evidence by any person disputing such fact.

2. And be it further enacted, that it shall be lawful to and for any person or persons, body or bodies politic or corporate, to accept and take any goods, wares, or merchandize, or the bill or bills of lading for the delivery thereof, in deposit or pledge, from any consignee or consignees thereof; but then and in that case such person or persons, body or bodies politic or corporate, shall acquire no further or other right, title, or interest, in or upon or to the said goods, wares, or merchandize, or any bill of lading for the delivery thereof, than was possessed, or could or might have been enforced by the said consignee or consignees at the time of such deposit or pledge as a security as aforesaid; but such person or persons, body or bodies politic or corporate, shall and may acquire, possess and enforce such right, title, or interest as was possessed, and might have been enforced, by such consignee or consignees, at the time of such deposit or pledge as aforesaid; any rule of law, usage or custom to the contrary notwithstanding.

3. Provided always, that nothing herein contained shall be deemed, construed, or taken to deprive or prevent the true owner or owners, proprietor or proprietors of such goods, wares, or merchandize, from demanding and recovering the same from his, her, or their factor or factors, agent or agents, before the same shall have been so deposited or pledged, or from the assignee or assignees of such factor or factors, agent or agents, in the event of his, her, or their bankruptcy; nor to prevent any such owner or owners, proprietor or proprietors, from demanding or recovering of and from any person or persons, or of or from the assignees of any person or persons in case of his or her bankruptcy, or of or from any body or bodies politic or corporate, such goods, wares, or

merchandize, so consigned, deposited or pledged, upon repayment of the money, or on restoration of the negotiable security or securities, or on payment of a sum of money equal to the amount of such security or securities, for which money or negotiable security or securities such person or persons, his, her, or their assignee or assignees, or such body or bodies politic or corporate, may be entitled to any lien upon such goods, wares, or merchandize; nor to prevent the said owner or owners, proprietor or proprietors, from recovering of and from such person or persons, body or bodies politic or corporate, any balance or sum of money remaining in his, her, or their hands, as the produce of the sale of such goods, wares, or merchandize, after deducting thereout the amount of the money or negotiable security or securities so advanced or given upon the security thereof as aforesaid: provided always, that in case of the bankruptcy of such factor or agent, the owner of the goods so pledged and redeemed as aforesaid shall be held to have discharged *pro tanto* the debt due by him to the bankrupt's estate.

---

6 GEO. 4, c. 94.

An Act to alter and amend an Act for the better Protection of the Property of Merchants and others, who may hereafter enter into Contracts or Agreements in relation to Goods, Wares, or Merchandize intrusted to Factors or Agents.

[5th July, 1825.]

" WHEREAS an Act passed in the fourth year of the reign of his present Majesty, intituled 'An Act for the better Protection of the Property of Merchants and others who may hereafter enter into Contracts or Agreements in relation to Goods, Wares, or Merchandize intrusted to Factors or Agents': and whereas it is expedient to alter and amend the said Act, and to make further provisions in relation to such contracts or agreements as hereinafter provided:" be it therefore enacted by the King's most excellent Majesty, by and with the advice and consent of the Lords spiritual and temporal, and Commons, in this present Parliament assembled, and by the authority of the same, that from and after the passing of this Act, any person or persons intrusted, for the purpose of consignment or of sale, with any goods, wares, or merchandize, and who shall have shipped such goods, wares, or merchandize in his, her, or their own name or names, and any person or persons in whose name or names any goods, wares, or merchandize shall be shipped by any other person or persons, shall be deemed and taken to be the true owner or owners thereof, so far as to entitle the consignee or consignees of such goods, wares, and merchandize to a lien thereon, in respect of any money or negotiable security or securities advanced or given by such consignee or consignees, to or for the use of the person or persons in whose name or names such goods, wares, or merchandize shall be shipped, or in respect of any money or negotiable security or securities received by him, her, or them, to the use of such consignee or consignees, in the like manner to all intents and purposes as if such person or persons was or were the true owner or owners of such goods, wares, and merchandize: provided such consignee or consignees shall not have notice by the bill of lading for the delivery of such goods, wares, or merchandize, or otherwise, at or before the time of any advance of such money or negotiable seecurity, or of such receipt of money or negotiable security in respect of which such lien is claimed, that such person or persons so shipping in his, her, or their own name or names, or in whose name or names any goods, wares, or merchandize shall be shipped by any person or persons, is or are not the actual and *bonâ fide* owner or owners, proprietor or proprietors of such goods, wares, and merchandize so shipped as aforesaid, any law, usage, or custom to the contrary thereof in any wise notwithstanding: provided also, that the person or persons in whose name or names any such goods, wares, or merchandize are so shipped as aforesaid, shall be taken, for the purposes of this Act, to have been intrusted therewith for the purpose of consignment or of sale, unless the contrary thereof shall be made to appear by bill of discovery or otherwise, or be made to appear, or be shown in evidence by any person disputing such fact.

2. And be it further enacted, that from and after the first day of October one thousand eight hundred and twenty-six, any person or persons intrusted with and in possession of any bill of lading, India warrant, dock warrant, warehousekeeper's certificate, wharfinger's certificate, warrant, or order for delivery of goods, shall be deemed and taken to be the true owner or owners of the goods, wares, and merchandize described and mentioned in the said several documents hereinbefore stated respectively, or either of them, so far as to give validity to any contract or agreement thereafter to be made or entered into by such person or persons so intrusted and in possession as aforesaid, with any person or persons, body or bodies politic or corporate, for the sale or disposition of the said goods, wares, and merchandize, or any part thereof, or for the deposit or pledge thereof or any part thereof, as a security for any money or negotiable instrument or instru-

ments advanced or given by such person or persons, body or bodies politic or corporate, upon the faith of such several documents or either of them : provided such person or persons, body or bodies politic or corporate, shall not have notice by such documents or either of them or otherwise, that such person or persons so intrusted as aforesaid is or are not the actual and *bona fide* owner or owners, proprietor or proprietors of such goods, wares, or merchandize so sold or deposited or pledged as aforesaid; any law, usage, or custom to the contrary thereof in any wise notwithstanding.

3. Provided always, and be it further enacted, that in case any person or persons, body or bodies politic or corporate, shall, after the passing of this Act, accept and take any such goods, wares, or merchandize in deposit or pledge from any such person or persons so in possession and intrusted as aforesaid, without notice as aforesaid, as a security for any debt or demand due and owing from such person or persons so intrusted and in possession as aforesaid, to such person or persons, body or bodies politic or corporate, before the time of such deposit or pledge, then and in that case such person or persons, body or bodies politic or corporate so accepting or taking such goods, wares, or merchandize in deposit or pledge, shall acquire no further or other right, title, or interest in or upon, or to the said goods, wares, or merchandize, or any such document as aforesaid, than was possessed or could or might have been enforced by the said person or persons so possessed and intrusted as aforesaid at the time of such deposit or pledge as a security as last aforesaid; but such person or persons, body or bodies politic or corporate, so accepting or taking such goods, wares or merchandize in deposit or pledge, shall and may acquire, possess and enforce such right, title or interest as was possessed and might have been enforced by such person or persons so possessed and intrusted as aforesaid; any rule of law, usage or custom to the contrary notwithstanding.

4. And be it further enacted, that from and after the first day of October one thousand eight hundred and twenty-six, it shall be lawful to and for any person or persons, body or bodies politic or corporate, to contract with any agent or agents, intrusted with any goods, wares or merchandize, or to whom the same may be consigned, for the purchase of any such goods, wares, and merchandize, and to receive the same of and pay for the same to such agent or agents; and such contract and payment shall be binding upon and good against the owner of such goods, wares, and merchandize notwithstanding such person or persons, body or bodies politic or corporate, shall have notice that the person or persons making and entering into such contract, or on whose behalf such con-

tract is made or entered into, is an agent or agents: provided such contract and payment be made in the usual and ordinary course of business, and that such person or persons, body or bodies politic or corporate shall not, when such contract is entered into or payment made, have notice that such agent or agents is or are not authorized to sell the said goods, wares, and merchandize, or to receive the said purchase-money.

5. And be it further enacted, that from and after the passing of this Act, it shall be lawful to and for any person or persons, body or bodies politic or corporate, to accept and take any such goods, wares, or merchandize, or any such document as aforesaid, in deposit or pledge from any such factor or factors, agent or agents, notwithstanding such person or persons, body or bodies politic or corporate, shall have such notice as aforesaid, that the person or persons making such deposit or pledge is or are a factor or factors, agent or agents; but then and in that case such person or persons, body or bodies politic or corporate, shall acquire no further or other right, title, or interest in or upon or to the said goods, wares, or merchandize, or on any such document as aforesaid, for the delivery thereof, than was possessed or could or might have been enforced by the said factor or factors, agent or agents, at the time of such deposit or pledge as a security as last aforesaid; but such person or persons, body or bodies politic or corporate, shall and may acquire, possess and enforce such right, title, or interest as was possessed and might have been enforced by such factor or factors, agent or agents, at the time of such deposit or pledge as aforesaid; any rule of law, usage or custom to the contrary notwithstanding.

6. Provided always, and be it enacted, that nothing herein contained shall be deemed, construed, or taken to deprive or prevent the true owner or owners, or proprietor or proprietors, of such goods, wares, or merchandize, from demanding and recovering the same from his, her, or their factor or factors, agent or agents, before the same shall have been so sold, deposited, or pledged, or from the assignee or assignees of such factor or factors, agent or agents, in the event of his, her, or their bankruptcy; nor to prevent such owner or owners, proprietor or proprietors, from demanding or recovering of and from any person or persons, body or bodies politic or corporate, the price or sum agreed to be paid for the purchase of such goods, wares, or merchandize, subject to any right of set-off on the part of such person or persons, body or bodies politic or corporate, against such factor or factors, agent or agents; nor to prevent such owner or owners, proprietor or proprietors, from demanding or recovering of and from such person or persons, body or bodies politic or corporate, such goods, wares, or merchandize so deposited or

pledged, upon repayment of the money, or on restoration of the negotiable instrument or instruments so advanced or given on the security of such goods, wares, or merchandize as aforesaid, by such person or persons, body or bodies politic or corporate to such factor or factors, agent or agents; and upon payment of such further sum of money, or on restoration of such other negotiable instrument or instruments (if any) as may have been advanced or given by such factor or factors, agent or agents, to such owner or owners, proprietor or proprietors, or on payment of a sum of money equal to the amount of such instrument or instruments; nor to prevent the said owner or owners, proprietor or proprietors, from recovering of and from such person or persons, body or bodies politic or corporate, any balance or sum of money remaining in his, her, or their hands, as the produce of the sale of such goods, wares, or merchandize, after deducting thereout the amount of the money or negotiable instrument or instruments so advanced or given upon the security thereof as aforesaid: provided always, that in case of the bankruptcy of any such factor or agent, the owner or owners, proprietor or proprietors of the goods, wares, and merchandize so pledged and redeemed as aforesaid, shall be held to have discharged *pro tanto* the debt due by him, her, or them to the estate of such bankrupt.

[*The remaining sections of this Act (i.e., ss. 7—10) are now superseded by the* 24 & 25 *Vict. c.* 96, *ss.* 78—79, 85, 86; *for which see Appendix,* No. 2, *ante p.* 75.]

---

5 & 6 VICT. c. 39.

An Act to amend the Law relating to Advances bonâ fide *made to Agents intrusted with Goods.*

[30th June, 1842.]

" WHEREAS by an Act passed in the sixth year of the reign of his late majesty King George the Fourth, intituled ' *An Act to alter and amend an Act for the better Protection of the Property of Merchants and others who may hereafter enter into Contracts or Agreements in relation to Goods, Wares and Merchandize intrusted to Factors or Agents;*' validity is given, under certain circumstances, to contracts or agreements made with persons intrusted with and in possession of the documents of title to goods and merchandize, and consignees making advances to persons abroad who are intrusted with any goods or merchandize are entitled, under certain circumstances, to a lien thereon, but under the said Act and the present state of the law advances cannot safely be made upon goods or documents to persons known to have possession thereof as agents only: And whereas by the said Act it is amongst other things further enacted, 'that it shall be lawful to and for any person to contract with any agent intrusted with any goods, or to whom the same may be consigned, for the purchase of any such goods, and to receive the same of and to pay for the same to such agent, and such contract and payment shall be binding upon and good against the owner of such goods, notwithstanding such person shall have notice that the person making such contract, or on whose behalf such contract is made, is an agent; provided such contract or payment be made in the usual and ordinary course of business, and that such person shall not, when such contract is entered into or payment made, have notice that such agent is not authorized to sell the same, or to receive the said purchase-money;' And whereas advances on the security of goods and merchandize have become an usual and ordinary course of business, and it is expedient and necessary that reasonable and safe facilities should be afforded thereto, and that the same protection and validity should be extended to *bonâ fide* advances upon goods and merchandize, as by the said recited Act is given to sales, and that owners intrusting agents with the possession of goods and merchandize, or of documents of title thereto, should in all cases where such owners by the said recited Act, or otherwise, would be bound by a contract or agreement of sale, be in like manner bound by any contract or agreement of pledge or lien for any advances *bonâ fide* made on the security thereof: And whereas much litigation has arisen on the construction of the said recited Act, and the same does not extend to protect exchanges of securities *bonâ fide* made, and so much uncertainty exists in respect thereof that it is expedient to alter and amend the same, and to extend the provisions thereof, and to put the law on a clear and certain basis:" be it therefore enacted by the Queen's most excellent Majesty, by and with the advice and consent of the Lords Spiritual and Temporal, and Commons, in this present parliament assembled, and by the authority of the same, That from and after the passing of this Act any agent who shall thereafter be intrusted with the possession of goods, or of the documents of title to goods, shall be deemed and taken to be owner of such goods and documents, so far as to give validity to any contract or agreement by way of pledge, lien, or security *bonâ fide* made by any person with such agent so intrusted as aforesaid, as well for any original loan, advance, or payment made upon the security of such goods or documents, as also for any further or continuing advance in respect thereof, and such contract or agreement shall be binding upon and good against the owner of such goods, and all other persons interested therein, notwithstanding the person claiming such pledge or lien may have had notice that the person with whom such contract or agreement is made is only an agent.

2. And be it enacted, that where any such contract or agreement for pledge, lien, or security shall be made in consideration of the delivery or transfer to such agent, of any other goods or merchandize, or document of title, or negotiable security, upon which the person so delivering up the same had at the time a valid and available lien and security for or in respect of a previous advance by virtue of some contract or agreement made with such agent, such contract and agreement, if *bonâ fide* on the part of the person with whom the same may be made, shall be deemed to be a contract made in consideration of an advance within the true intent and meaning of this Act, and shall be as valid and effectual, to all intents and purposes, and to the same extent, as if the consideration for the same had been a *bonâ fide* present advance of money: Provided always, that the lien acquired under such last-mentioned contract or agreement, upon the goods or documents deposited in exchange, shall not exceed the value at the time, of the goods and merchandize which, or documents of title to which, or the negotiable security which shall be delivered up and exchanged.

3. Provided always, and be it enacted, that this Act, and every matter and thing herein contained, shall be deemed and construed to give validity to such contracts and agreements only, and to protect only such loans, advances, and exchanges, as shall be made *bonâ fide*, and without notice that the agent making such contracts or agreements as aforesaid has not authority to make the same, or is acting *malâ fide* in respect thereof against the owner of such goods and merchandize; and nothing herein contained shall be construed to extend to or protect, any lien or pledge for or in respect of any antecedent debt, owing from any agent to any person with or to whom such lien or pledge shall be given, nor to authorize any agent intrusted as aforesaid in deviating from any express orders or authority received from the owner; but that, for the purpose and to the intent of protecting all such *bonâ fide* loans, advances, and exchanges as aforesaid (though made with notice of such agent not being the owner, but without any notice of the agent's acting without authority), and to no further or other intent or purpose, such contract or agreement as aforesaid shall be binding on the owner and all other persons interested in such goods.

4. And be it enacted, that any bill of lading, India warrant,

dock warrant, warehouse keeper's certificate, warrant, or order for the delivery of goods, or any other document used in the ordinary course of business as proof of the possession or control of goods, or authorizing or purporting to authorize, either by indorsement or by delivery, the possessor of such document to transfer or receive goods thereby represented, shall be deemed and taken to be a document of title within the meaning of this Act; and any agent intrusted as aforesaid, and possessed of any such document of title, whether derived immediately from the owner of such goods, or obtained by reason of such agent's having been intrusted with the possession of the goods, or of any other document of title thereto, shall be deemed and taken to have been intrusted with the possession of the goods represented by such document of title as aforesaid, and all contracts pledging or giving a lien upon such document of title as aforesaid, shall be deemed and taken to be respectively pledges of and liens upon the goods to which the same relates; and such agent shall be deemed to be possessed of such goods or documents, whether the same shall be in his actual custody, or shall be held by any other person subject to his control or for him or on his behalf; and where any loan or advance shall be *bonâ fide* made to any agent intrusted with, and in possession of, any such goods or documents of title as aforesaid, on the faith of any contract or agreement in writing to consign, deposit, transfer, or deliver such goods or documents of title as aforesaid, and such goods or documents of title shall actually be received by the person making such loan or advance, without notice that such agent was not authorized to make such pledge or security, every such loan or advance, shall be deemed and taken to be a loan or advance on the security of such goods or documents of title within the meaning of this Act, though such goods or documents of title shall not actually be received by the person making such loan or advance till the period subsequent thereto; and any contract or agreement, whether made direct with such agent as aforesaid, or with any clerk or other person on his behalf, shall be deemed a contract or agreement with such agent; and any payment made, whether by money or bills of exchange, or other negotiable security, shall be deemed and taken to be an advance within the meaning of this Act; and an agent in possession as aforesaid of such goods or documents shall be taken, for the purposes of this Act, to have been intrusted therewith by the owner thereof, unless the contrary can be shown in evidence.

5. Provided always, and be it enacted, that nothing herein contained shall lessen, vary, alter, or affect the civil responsibility of an agent for any breach of duty or contract, or non-

fulfilment of his orders or authority in respect of any such contract, agreement, lien, or pledge as aforesaid.

[*Section 6 is now superseded by the* 24 & 25 *Vict. c.* 96, *ss.* 78, 85; for which see Appendix, No. 2, *ante,* p. 75.]

7. Provided also, and be it enacted, that nothing herein contained shall prevent such owner as aforesaid, from having the right to redeem such goods or documents of title pledged as aforesaid, at any time before such goods shall have been sold, upon repayment of the amount of the lien thereon, or restoration of the securities in respect of which such lien may exist, and upon payment or satisfaction to such agent, if by him required, of any sum of money for or in respect of which such agent would by law be entitled to retain the same goods or documents, or any of them, by way of lien as against such owner, or to prevent the said owner from recovering of and from such person with whom any such goods or documents may have been pledged, or who shall have any such lien thereon as aforesaid, any balance or sum of money remaining in his hands as the produce of the sale of such goods, after deducting the amount of the lien of such person under such contract or agreement as aforesaid: Provided always, that in case of the bankruptcy of any such agent, the owner of the goods which shall have been so redeemed by such owner as aforesaid shall, in respect of the sum paid by him on account of such agent for such redemption, be held to have paid such sum for the use of such agent before his bankruptcy, or in case the goods shall not be so redeemed, the owner shall be deemed a creditor of such agent for the value of the goods so pledged at the time of the pledge, and shall, if he shall think fit, be entitled in either of such cases to prove for or set off the sum so paid, or the value of such goods, as the case may be.

8. And be it enacted, that in construing this Act the word "person" shall be taken to designate a body corporate, or company, as well as an individual; and that words in the singular number shall, when necessary to give effect to the intention of the said Act, import also the plural, and *vice versa;* and words used in the masculine gender shall, when required, be taken to apply to a female as well as a male.

9. Provided also, and be it enacted, that nothing herein contained shall be construed to give validity to, or in anywise to affect any contract, agreement, lien, pledge, or other act, matter, or thing made or done before the passing of this Act.

THE FACTORS ACTS, 1823—1877.   89

40 & 41 VICT. c. 39.

An Act to amend the Factors' Acts.

[10th August, 1877.]

WHEREAS doubts have arisen with respect to the true meaning of certain provisions of the Factors' Acts, and it is expedient to remove such doubts and otherwise to amend the said Acts, for the better security of persons buying or making advances on goods, or documents of title to goods, in the usual and ordinary course of mercantile business:

Be it enacted by the Queen's most excellent Majesty, by and with the advice and consent of the Lords spiritual and temporal, and Commons, in this present Parliament assembled, and by the authority of the same, as follows:

1. In this Act, the expression "the principal Acts" means the following Acts; that is to say,

The Act of the 4th Geo. IV. (1823), c. 83.
The Act of the 6th Geo. IV. (1825), c. 94.
The Act of the 5th and 6th of her Majesty (1842), c. 39.

And the said Acts and this Act may be cited for all purposes as the "Factors' Acts, 1823 to 1877."

2. Where any agent or person has been intrusted with and continues in the possession of any goods, or documents of title to goods, within the meaning of the principal Acts as amended by this Act, any revocation of his intrustment or agency shall not prejudice or affect the title or rights of any other person who, without notice of such revocation, purchases such goods, or makes advances upon the faith or security of such goods or documents.

3. Where any goods have been sold, and the vendor or any person on his behalf continues or is in possession of the documents of title thereto, any sale, pledge, or other disposition of the goods or documents made by such vendor or any person or agent intrusted by the vendor with the goods or documents within the meaning of the principal Acts as amended by this Act so continuing or being in possession, shall be as valid and effectual as if such vendor or person were an agent or person intrusted by the vendee with the goods or documents within the meaning of the principal Acts as amended by this Act, provided the person to whom the sale, pledge, or other disposition is made has not notice that the goods have been previously sold.

4. Where any goods have been sold or contracted to be sold, and the vendee, or any person on his behalf, obtains the possession of the documents of title thereto from the vendor or his agents, any sale, pledge, or disposition of such goods or documents by such vendee so in possession or by any other

person or agent intrusted by the vendee with the documents within the meaning of the principal Acts as amended by this Act shall be as valid and effectual as if such vendee or other person were an agent or person intrusted by the vendor with the documents within the meaning of the principal Acts as amended by this Act, provided the person to whom the sale, pledge, or other disposition is made has not notice of any lien or other right of the vendor in respect of the goods.

5. Where any document of title to goods has been lawfully indorsed or otherwise transferred to any person as a vendee or owner of the goods, and such person transfers such document by indorsement (or by delivery where the document is by custom, or by its express terms transferable by delivery, or makes the goods deliverable to the bearer) to a person who takes the same *bonâ fide* and for valuable consideration, the last-mentioned transfer shall have the same effect for defeating any vendor's lien or right of stoppage *in transitu* as the transfer of a bill of lading has for defeating the right of stoppage *in transitu*.

6. This Act shall apply only to acts done and rights acquired after the passing of this Act.

INDEX.

ADVANCE,
    actual money, necessary for validity of pledge under Factors Act, 1842..35, 51.
    pecuniary liability incurred by pledgee, a good consideration in lieu of an, under Factors Act, 1889..35.
    further or continuing, need not be made to the same person to whom the original advance was made, 35.
    must be made *bonâ fide*, 39.
    colourable, which is only a means of relieving pledgee from liability, not protected, 39.
    the *bonâ fides* of an, question for the jury, 39.
    made to agent without notice that his authority has been revoked, is protected, 40.
    factor or agent unlawfully obtaining, Appendix II., 75. And see *Criminal Liability.*

AGENT,
    description of, under the earlier Factors Acts, 11, 22.
    must be a factor or agent to whose employment a power of sale is incident, 11.
    interpretation of "agent intrusted" under earlier Factors Acts, 13, 23.
    must have received possession of goods for purpose of sale or for some object connected therewith, 14, 22.
    mercantile, definition of, given by Factors Act, 21.
    no longer required to be "intrusted" by Factors Act, 22.
    but must have a prescribed authority, 23.
    must be in possession of goods as agent, 24.
    must be a mercantile agent, 24.
    invested by Factors Act with a statutory authority superadded to authority conferred by principal, 24.
    under the Factors Act does not include warehouseman or wharfinger, 31.
        nor clerk, servant, cashier, caretaker, &c., 31.
        nor carrier or forwarding agent, 31.
    civil and criminal liability of, preserved by 12th section of the Factors Act, 1889..69.
    carrying on business in two characters and intended only in one, 13, 26.
    common law powers of, unaffected by the Factors Act, 71. And see *Agent Intrusted; Factor;* and *Mercantile Agent.*

AGENT INTRUSTED AND IN POSSESSION,
    judicial interpretation of the term under the earlier Factors Acts, 13.
    the Factors Act, 1889, substitutes a mercantile agent having prescribed authority for, 22.
    submitted that change of language has not effected a change in the law, 25. And see *Intrustment.*

INDEX.

ANTECEDENT DEBT OR LIABILITY,
  pledge by mercantile agent in respect of, 43.
  what constitutes, 47 *et seq.*
  decision under the previous Factors Act with reference to, 47.

APPARENT OR OSTENSIBLE OWNERSHIP,
  doctrine of, 8.
  confined by the earlier Factors Acts to the case of persons dealing with mercantile agents, 9.
  extended under Factors Act, 1877, to the case of seller or buyer in possession of a document of title, 17.
    re-enacted by Factors Act, 1889..57 *et seq.*

AUCTIONEER,
  does Factors Act apply to, 27, n. (*g*).

BARTER,
  factor at common law not permitted to, 39, 51.
  but empowered by the 5th section of the Factors Act, 1889..39, 51.

BILL OF LADING,
  factor could not pledge previous to Factors Acts, 4.
  a document of title under Factors Acts, 32.
  effect of transfer of, 33, 66, 67.
    See also *Document of Title.*

BONA FIDES,
  of person dealing with agent, 39.
  of transfer of a document of title, 66.
  only requires that transferee is without notice of circumstances rendering bill of lading not fairly and honestly assignable, 64.

BROKER,
  definition of, 29.
  statutory definition of mercantile agent includes, when in possession of goods or of documents of title which he is employed to sell or buy, 29.
  when in possession of goods about which he is employed, is, strictly speaking, a factor, and has implied authority to sell or pledge them, 25.
  for purchase of goods, had at common law implied authority to sell them if left in his possession, 29.
  employed to raise money upon the security of goods or of documents of title, 30.
  in possession of goods about which he is employed has same lien as a factor, 44.

BUYER,
  allowed to obtain possession of a document of title not within operation of earlier Factors Acts, 11, 16, 69.
  law altered by Factors Act, 1877..17.
  dispositions by, obtaining possession of goods bought or of documents of title under Factors Act, 1889..60 *et seq.*

CASH RECEIPT,
  transfer of, not equivalent to that of a delivery order, 68.

INDEX.

CLERK OR SERVANT,
    not an agent within Factors Acts, 31.
    if authorized in ordinary course of business may contract on agent's behalf, 54.

CONSIGNEE,
    Factors Act, 1823, applied only to, 9.
    enabled to transfer lien for advances, 9.
    confirmed by Factors Act, 1825..9.
    lien of, under 7th section of Factors Act, 1889..54.

CONSIGNOR,
    for sale, within statutory definition of mercantile agent, 21, 25.
    foreign, right of, to recover goods, 71.

CRIMINAL LIABILITY,
    of factor or agent under Larceny Act, 1861, Appendix No. II., 75.
    of agent, preserved by 12th section of Factors Act, 1889..69.

DELEGATION OF AGENT'S AUTHORITY,
    not permitted at common law without principal's assent, 54.
    under 6th section of Factors Act, 1889..54.

DELIVERY ORDER,
    a document of title within definition of Factors Act, 1889..32.
    effect of transfer of, at common law, 33, 66.
    delivery of goods not complete until the bailee attorned to the buyer, 66.
    transfer of, from a buyer to a sub-purchaser, did not at common law divest seller's lien, 67.
    transfer of, contrasted with that of a bill of lading, 67.
    custom of merchants with reference to transfer of, 67.
    effect of 10th section of the Factors Act, 1889, upon the transfer of, 68.
    transfer of, by buyer to sub-purchaser or pledgee divests in whole or in part the original seller's rights, 68.
        aliter as between seller and buyer, 68.
    See also *Document of Title*.

DISPOSITION OF GOODS,
    under Factors Act, 1825, must be in the nature of a sale or pledge, 38.
    will include barter under Factors Act, 1889..39.

DOCK WARRANT,
    a document of title as defined by Factors Act, 1889..32.
    common law conception of, 33, 67.
    effect of transfer of, independently of Factors Acts, 33, 67.
        under Factors Act, 1889..65 *et seq.*
        by agent entrusted with bill of lading, 42.
    And see *Document of Title*.

DOCUMENT OF TITLE,
    definition of, in Factors Acts, 32.
    includes bill of lading, dock warrant, warehouse-keeper's certificate, warrant or order for delivery of goods, 32.
    statutory and common law interpretation of, 33, 67.
    practice of merchants with regard to, 33, 67.

DOCUMENT OF TITLE—*continued.*
    effect of Factors Act, 1877, upon transfer of, 34.
    question whether a wharfinger's certificate is or is not a, 34.
    recent cases upon the construction of trade documents alleged to be documents of title, 34, n. (*k*).
    possession by agent of a "derivative," 41.
    primâ facie presumption that he is in possession with the owner's consent, 42.
    a pledge of, deemed to be a pledge of the goods, 43.
    seller allowed to remain in possession of, not an "agent intrusted" therewith under Factors Act, 1825..11, 16, 57.
    law altered by Factors Act, 1877, and re-enacted by Factors Act, 1889..17, 57.
    buyer allowed to obtain possession of, not an "agent intrusted" therewith under Factors Act, 1825..11, 16, 61.
    law altered by Factors Act, 1877, and re-enacted by Factors Act, 1889..17, 60.
    transfer of, from a buyer to *bonâ fide* sub-purchaser or pledgee, 62 *et seq.*
    variance between the 9th and 10th sections of the Factors Act, 1889, on this point, 63.
    transferor of, must have a title to the goods represented by the document, 65.
    transfer of, may be by indorsement or by delivery under 11th section of Factors Act, 1889..69.
        And see *Bill of Lading*; *Delivery Order*; *Dock Warrant*; *Wharfinger's Certificate.*

ESTOPPEL,
    doctrine of, 8.
    Factors Acts based upon, 9, 17.
    did not apply to the case of a seller or buyer in possession of goods, or of documents of title, 57, 61.
    law altered by Factors Act, 1877, and re-enacted by Factors Act, 1889..57 *et seq.*

EXCHANGE OF SECURITIES,
    by factor, not protected by Factors Act, 1825..50, 52.
        protected by Factors Act, 1842..50, 53.
        Factors Act, 1889, confirms this provision, 53.
    lien on goods or documents of title deposited in exchange not to exceed value of those given up, 53.
    agent depositing goods or documents of title in exchange not necessarily the original pledgor, 53.

FACTOR,
    definitions of, 28.
    at common law had authority to sell but not to pledge, 3.
    the rule laid down in *Paterson* v. *Tash*, 3.
    decisions before the Factors Acts on factor's power to pledge, 5, n. (*q*).
    first conferred by Factors Act, 1842..12.
    implied authority of, 28.
    term includes commission agent and assignee for sale, 29.
    may also be consignor of goods, 29.

INDEX. 95

FACTOR—*continued.*
dispositions by, in possession of goods or of documents of title with owner's consent, 36 *et seq.* See *Pledge* and *Sale.*
pledge by, for antecedent debt or liability, 43.
lien of, its nature, 44.
    what constitutes, 45 *et seq.*
pledge by, whose authority has been revoked, 40.
    of a "derivative" document of title, 41.
exchange of securities by, 49 *et seq.*
conditional lien for, under liability for acceptances, 46.
submitted that he can transfer a conditional lien, 46.
bankruptcy of, rights of owner on, 69 *et seq.*
criminal liability of, under Larceny Act, 1861, Appendix No. II., 75.
And see *Agent* and *Mercantile Agent.*

FACTORS ACTS,
origin and history of, 3 *et seq.*
change of law and policy involved in, 6.
Factors Act, 1823 (4 Geo. IV. c. 83), 9.
    1825 (6 Geo. IV. c. 94), 9—12.
    1842 (5 & 6 Vict. c. 39), 12—16.
    1877 (40 & 41 Vict. c. 39), 16—18.
    1889 (52 & 53 Vict. c. 45), 19 *et seq.*
        amendments contained in, 19.
        summary of its provisions, 20.
For the text of the Factors Acts, 1823—1877, see Appendix No. III., 78.

FRANCE,
law of, with relation to title to moveables, originally based upon the civil law, 7.
afterwards adopted the doctrine that "possession constitutes title," 8.
provisions of the Code Napoléon, Appendix No. I., 73.

FRAUD,
consent of owner to agent's possession obtained by, 37.

FURNITURE
in a furnished house not "goods" within meaning of the Factors Acts, 32, n. (*d*).

GERMANY,
provisions of the commercial code of, relating to title to moveables, Appendix No. I., 73.

GOODS,
definition of, in Factors Act, 32.
restricted to merchandise, 32.
will not include furniture in a furnished house, 32, n. (*d*).
sale of. See *Sale of Goods.*

GUARANTOR,
exchange of securities by a, 53.

HOUSE OF COMMONS,
inquiry of committee of, into law and practice relating to factor's power to pledge, 5 *et seq.*

INDEX.

INDIA WARRANT,
no longer included as a document of title under Factors Act, 1889..33.

INTRUSTMENT,
limiting signification attached to the expression by the Courts, 13, 23.
possession by agent only raised *primâ facie* presumption of, under Factors Act, 1842..14.
effect of Factors Act, 1889..22 *et seq.* And see *Agent Intrusted and in Possession.*

LIABILITY,
pecuniary, incurred by pledgee, good consideration for pledge under Factors Act, 1889..35.
pledge made in respect of antecedent, 43 *et seq.*
what constitutes an antecedent, 47.
decisions under previous Factors Act reviewed, 47.

LIEN,
of consignee under Factors Acts, 1823 and 1825..9.
is transferable, 9.
factor's, nature of, 44.
  not transferable at common law, 45.
  what constitutes, 45.
  submitted that it now includes factor's liability under acceptances, 46.
  will not include a mere money claim unless general balance of account in factor's favour, 46.
vendor's. See *Vendor's Lien.*

LOAN. See *Advance.*

MARKET OVERT,
sale of goods in, 8.

MERCANTILE AGENT,
definition of, for the purposes of the Factors Act, 1889..21.
principal classes of, 27.
Mr. Justice Story's classification, 27, n. (*q*).
disposition by, 36 *et seq.*
in possession of goods or documents of title with owner's consent, substituted for " agent intrusted," of the earlier Factors Acts, 25, 37.
disposition by, whose authority has been secretly revoked, 40.
possession by, of " derivative" document of title, 41.
pledge by, for antecedent debt or liability, 43.
And see *Agent* and *Factor.*

NEGOTIABLE INSTRUMENT,
pledge of, valid independently of Factors Acts, 31.
  Factors Act, 1889, does not affect, 53.

NOTICE,
person dealing with mercantile agent must have no, of agent's want of authority, 36.
what constitutes, left to ordinary rules of evidence, 40.

INDEX. 97

NOTICE—*continued.*
    may be actual or constructive, 40.
        verbal or in writing, 40.
    rule as to, laid down by Lord Tenterden, 40.
    modern tendency to limit doctrine of construction, 40.
    doubtful how far distinguishable from knowledge, 40.
    mere suspicion of agent's want of authority is insufficient, 40.
    of pledgor's agency, no longer invalidates a pledge in respect of an antecedent debt or liability, 44.
    by consignee, that consignor is not owner, 56.
    by second buyer or pledgee, of previous sale, 69.

OWNER OF GOODS,
    under Factors Act, 1842, might rebut presumption of intrustment, 14, 25.
    consent of, to agent's possession necessary, 37, 42.
        obtained by agent's fraud, 37.
    right of, to redeem goods or recover their proceeds from agent or person claiming under a disposition from the agent, 70, 71.
    foreign principal may avail himself of the 12th section of the Factors Act, 1889..71.

PARTNER,
    question whether the Factors Act applies to, 27, n (*g*).

PERSON,
    interpretation of term in earlier Factors Acts as agent, 11, 16, 23.
    includes any body of persons, corporate or unincorporate, 36.

PLEDGE,
    factor no power to, before Factors Acts, 3.
        cases decided thereon, 5, n. (*g*).
    factor's power to, first conferred by Factors Act, 1842..12.
    authority to, placed by Factors Act, 1889, on same footing with authority to sell, 25.
    agent's power to, not exhausted by first pledge, 32.
    definition of, in Factors Act, 1889..35.
    a money advance necessary consideration for, under Factors Act, 1842..35.
    a pecuniary liability incurred by pledgee a valid consideration for, under Factors Act, 1889..35.
    by mercantile agent in possession of goods or documents of title with owner's consent, 36.
        now assumed to be within ordinary business of a mercantile agent, 39.
    of documents of title deemed to be a pledge of the goods, 43.
    for antecedent debt or liability, 43 *et seq.*
    valid to extent of agent's lien enforceable at time of pledge, 43.
    for antecedent debt, Factors Act, 1889, repeals proviso as to notice of pledgor's agency contained in Factors Act, 1825..44.
        and extends protection to an antecedent liability which was excluded from Factors Act, 1825..44.
    must be made to the same person to whom the pledgor is already indebted or liable, 49.

PLEDGE—*continued*.
    valid consideration for, defined, 49.
    by seller continuing or being in possession of goods sold, or of documents of title relating thereto, 56 *et seq*.
    by buyer obtaining possession of goods bought, or of documents of title relating thereto, 60 *et seq*.
    of a bill of lading, effect upon seller's right of stoppage *in transitu*, 66.
    seller entitled to surplus proceeds of sale after satisfying pledgee's claim, 66.

POSSESSION,
    only *primâ facie* evidence of intrustment under Factors Act, 1842.. 13, 23.
    of goods or documents of title by mercantile agent must be with owner's consent under Factors Act, 1889..36.
    only *primâ facie* evidence of owner's consent thereto, 37, 42.
    of agent obtained by fraud, 37.
    actual custody of goods or documents of title not necessary, 31.
    by another person subject to the agent's control, and on his behalf, sufficient, 32.
    of a document of title derived from possession of goods or of another document, 41.
    seller or buyer continuing in, or obtaining, of goods or of a document of title, 11, 16, 56 *et seq*.

POSSESSION CONSTITUTES TITLE (*POSSESSION VAUT TITRE*),
    doctrine adopted by commercial nations of Europe with regard to moveables, 8.

REDEMPTION,
    right of, by owner of goods, 69.

REVOCATION OF AUTHORITY,
    secret, of agent, does not affect title of *bonâ fide* purchaser or pledgee, 40.

SALE OF GOODS,
    by factor under 4th section of Factors Act, 1825..10.
        apparently only confirmatory of the common law, 10.
    by mercantile agent under Factors Act, 1889..36 *et seq*.
    valid consideration for, defined, 49.
    by seller, continuing or being in possession of goods sold or of a document of title thereto, 56.
    by buyer, allowed to obtain possession of goods bought or of a document of title thereto, 60.
    unnecessary that there should be a memorandum of contract to satisfy Statute of Frauds, 60.
    effect of, by buyer, accompanied by transfer of a document of title upon original seller's rights, 65.

SCOTLAND,
    by law of, possession of moveables constitutes title, 8.
    Factors Act, 1889, does not apply to, 72.

SELLER,
    allowed to remain in possession of a document of title not within the operation of the earlier Factors Acts, 11, 16.
    disposition by, continuing or being in possession of goods or of documents of title, 56 *et seq.*
        not provided for by the three earliest Factors Acts, 57.
    Factors Act, 1889, substantially re-enacts Factors Act, 1877, on this point, 58.
    particulars in which it amends the law, 58, 59.

SET-OFF,
    buyer may set-off a debt due from the factor to himself against the price, 51, n. (*n*).
    buyer or consignee may set-off any claim upon the agent against the principal's demand for the goods, 71.

SHIPMENT,
    of goods in consignor's name, 55.

STOPPAGE *IN TRANSITU*,
    effect of transfer of bill of lading upon right of, 65.
    seller's right of, defeated in whole or in part by transfer of a document of title from a buyer to a *bonâ fide* sub-purchaser or pledgee, 65 *et seq.*
    as affected by a sub-sale during transit, 66.
        by a pledge, 66.
    not defeated by transfer of cash receipts to a sub-purchaser, 68.

SUSPICION
    of agency does not invalidate disposition, 40.

TITLE,
    to goods, rule of English common law that no one can give a better, than he himself possesses, 7.
    exceptions to this rule, 8.
    possession constitutes, rule of commercial nations of Europe, 8.
    document of. See *Document of Title.*

VENDOR'S LIEN,
    divested in whole or in part by the transfer of a document of title from a buyer to a *bonâ fide* purchaser or pledgee, 60, 65.
    not divested by the transfer of a delivery order or dock-warrant from seller to buyer, 62.
    otherwise by the transfer of a bill of lading, 62, 64.

WAREHOUSEMAN,
    not an agent within the meaning of the earlier Factors Acts, although he also carry on business as a factor, 11, 13.
        nor within the statutory definition of a mercantile agent in Factors Act, 1889..26.

WAREHOUSE-KEEPER'S CERTIFICATE,
    a document of title as defined by the Factors Act, 1889..32. See *Document of Title.*

WARRANT,
    a document of title as defined by the Factors Act, 1889..32. And see *Dock-Warrant ; Document of Title*.

WHARFINGER,
    not an agent within the meaning of the earlier Factors Acts, although he also carry on business as a factor, 11, 13.
    law not altered by the Factors Act, 1889..26.

WHARFINGER'S CERTIFICATE,
    not specified as a document of title under Factors Act, 1889..32.
    whether or not document of title will depend upon its form, 34. See *Document of Title*.

THE END.

www.ingramcontent.com/pod-product-compliance
Lightning Source LLC
Chambersburg PA
CBHW030410170426
43202CB00010B/1554